"Whether you believe in passive investing or active management, this book offers something for everyone. The practical advice and personal stories in the book serve as a guide and a source of motivation, encouraging readers to embark on their own investment journeys."

Christopher Tan,
CEO and Founder of Providend Ltd

"I was hooked by the sharp writings of *Invest Lah!* I bought the book years ago when it was first released. I was so excited to share it with my dad who trades stocks, because I knew it would be simple to read and understand.

"Ser Jing, Sudhan and Wei Lin's writings are clear and succinct. It felt like a conversation with wise friends who know the terrain well — and want to make sure you don't fall into the same potholes.

"My favourite section? Mistakes Made and Lessons Learned by the authors. I've gained so much from just reading their past investing experiences. After investing for over 14 years, I still believe it's always better to learn from other people's mistakes.

"If you're getting your feet wet into the deep world of stock investing, I'd highly recommend this book. It's honest, practical and written by investors who walk the talk."

Willie Keng, CFA,
Founder of DividendTitan.com

Tenth Anniversary | Special Edition

INVEST LAH!

The Average Joe's Guide to Investing

Tenth Anniversary | Special Edition

INVEST LAH!

The Average Joe's Guide to Investing

Ser Jing Chong
Sudhan s/o Purushothuman
Wei Lin Ting

World Scientific

NEW JERSEY • LONDON • SINGAPORE • BEIJING • SHANGHAI • HONG KONG • TAIPEI • CHENNAI • TOKYO

Published by

World Scientific Publishing Co. Pte. Ltd.
5 Toh Tuck Link, Singapore 596224
USA office: 27 Warren Street, Suite 401-402, Hackensack, NJ 07601
UK office: 57 Shelton Street, Covent Garden, London WC2H 9HE

British Library Cataloguing-in-Publication Data
A catalogue record for this book is available from the British Library.

INVEST LAH!
The Average Joe's Guide to Investing — Tenth Anniversary Special Edition

ISBN 978-981-98-1505-0 (hardcover)
ISBN 978-981-98-1576-0 (paperback)
ISBN 978-981-98-1506-7 (ebook for institutions)
ISBN 978-981-98-1507-4 (ebook for individuals)

For any available supplementary material, please visit
https://www.worldscientific.com/worldscibooks/10.1142/14363#t=suppl

Desk Editor: Nicole Ong

Disclaimer

This publication contains the opinions and ideas of its respective contributors. It is not a recommendation to purchase or sell the products, services, shares, stocks, projects, programmes or franchises of any of the companies or investments herein discussed. This publication is sold with the understanding that the authors and publisher are not engaged in rendering legal, accounting, investments or other professional services.

The opinions and views expressed by the authors and contributors in this book are solely their own and do not necessarily represent the official views or professional capacity of any organisations they may be affiliated with.

As laws and regulations vary from country to country, should the reader require expert financial or other assistance or legal service, a competent professional should be consulted. Neither the authors nor the publisher can guarantee the accuracy of the information contained herein. The authors and publisher specifically disclaim any responsibility for any liability, loss or risk, personal or otherwise, which is incurred as a consequence, directly or indirectly, from attending any training programmes or investing in any products, services, franchises or business mentioned in this book or that which arising from the use and application of any of the contents of this book.

About the Authors

Ser Jing is the Portfolio Manager and co-founder of Compounder Fund. Ser Jing graduated with honours in 2012 from the National University of Singapore's Engineering Science Programme. But having been bitten by the investing bug since he was in his late teens, he decided to pursue a career in the investing world.

From January 2013 to October 2019, Ser Jing served in Motley Fool Singapore as a writer as well as a co-leader of the investing team. One of his career highlights with Fool Singapore was to help its flagship investment newsletter, Stock Advisor Gold, outperform a global stock market benchmark by nearly 2× over a 3.5-year period.

Ser Jing has been helping his family invest since October 2010, and is also the co-author of a popular Singapore-themed investment book *Invest Lah! The Average Joe's Guide To Investing*. When he's not busy digging through company reports, writing about his thoughts on investing, or actually investing, he can be found diving, playing music, exercising, meditating, playing football, and spending quality time with his loved ones.

Sudhan is a passionate investor who's been investing in the stock market since 2009. He is a huge advocate of investor education and believes in the act of paying it forward.

He co-authored the best-selling Singapore-themed stock market investment book, *Invest Lah! The Average Joe's Guide to Investing* in 2014 together with Ser Jing and Wei Lin to help fellow Singaporeans learn about investing.

He has also been featured on traditional media platforms such as 938NOW, Money FM 89.3, Oli 96.8FM, and Tamil Murasu discussing personal finance and investing.

Currently, Sudhan is with the advisory team at Providend, Singapore's sole fee-only comprehensive wealth advisory firm. Previously, he has held roles at The Motley Fool Singapore, Seedly, Google, and Endowus.

During his free time, Sudhan runs an investing newsletter at TheCompoundingDad.com, where he helps readers make smarter investment decisions through actionable and simple-to-understand content.

Sudhan graduated with a BSc (Hons) in Aircraft Engineering from Kingston University London.

Wei Lin is the co-founder and CEO of WhatsApp Quiz Maker by JoyfulPerson — the fastest way to train your workforce. The founding team has successfully scaled WhatsApp Quiz Maker to more than 84 countries worldwide, empowering companies with simple, scalable, and effective training tools.

Former government scholar turned entrepreneur, Wei Lin is the co-owner of businesses in software, F&B and fitness. He is also the co-author of *Invest Lah*, a best-selling business and investment book in Kinokuniya and Times Bookstore.

As an avid believer in giving back to the community, Wei Lin is the founding chairperson for NTU's SPMS Youth Expedition Team, he has led and participated in expedition teams to SEA countries for community service.

During his free time, he enjoys basketball, singing and hunting for the most authentic food from around the world.

Foreword

I felt very honoured when Ser Jing and Sudhan asked me to write the foreword of their book. I took a long time to submit my draft, partly because of my busy work in the office and at home, but largely because I wanted to make sure I at least go through the book very quickly to ensure I know what the book is all about.

After reading through the book, I found myself genuinely impressed. The clarity of explanations was notable and the book is simple enough to understand for new investors, while also providing useful insights for seasoned traders to understand what investing is really about. Ser Jing, Sudhan, and Wei Lin have effectively broken down complex concepts into digestible parts. In this new edition, they interviewed various types of investors, including investment educators, researchers, a financial influencer, fund managers, private investors, and myself, a wealth adviser. These interviews offer a range of perspectives, providing readers with a comprehensive view of investing.

All of us have different approaches to investing, which gives readers different perspectives on how people invest. However, our objectives are the same — to beat inflation and accumulate sufficient wealth to fund our life goals. This shared goal connects us, even though our methods may differ. The book aptly highlights these differences and similarities, offering a balanced view of the investment landscape.

A few months before Ser Jing interviewed me for this book, we had lunch together. We shared our views and approaches to investing.

I am of the opinion that most of the time, active managers cannot outperform the markets. For those who can, they often struggle to do so consistently. Ser Jing, on the other hand, runs the Compounder Fund which engages in security selection, a form of active management. Our discussion was enlightening, and I was inspired by his dedication. While I use my investment returns to fund my ikigai goals, Ser Jing finds ikigai from managing his fund. Ikigai is a Japanese word that means "doing things that are worthy in your daily living". This conversation gave me a deeper understanding of why he still actively manages his portfolio.

Whether you believe in passive investing or active management, this book offers something for everyone. It not only teaches you how to invest but also inspires you to start if you haven't already. The practical advice and personal stories in the book serve as a guide and a source of motivation, encouraging readers to embark on their own investment journeys.

Enjoy the book. I believe it will be a valuable addition to your financial education and an inspiration for your investment efforts.

Christopher Tan
CEO and Founder of Providend Ltd

Contents

Our Introduction

It's hard to believe that a decade has flown by since we first published *Invest Lah! The Average Joe's Guide to Investing* in 2014. What started as an attempt to demystify investing in Singapore has humbly garnered the attention and support of the investing public.

To mark the occasion, we wanted to bring together a group of people from the Singapore investing community.

What you have in your hands is the culmination of this effort: a compilation of interviews with seven established investors conducted between 2023 and 2024. Each of these individuals has generously shared their unique experiences, strategies, and perspectives on navigating the ever-evolving financial landscape.

The last few years have been particularly instructive for investors, shaped by the unprecedented challenges of the COVID-19 pandemic and the ensuing market volatility. As we may know, market turmoil is a feature of the stock market, not a bug. The insights shared by these investors shed light on how they adapted to these disruptions and reaffirm the enduring relevance of sound investing principles. We believe these interviews are timeless, just like the investing concepts we introduced in the original *Invest Lah*.

This 10th Anniversary Edition is more than just a celebration; it's also a way for us to give back. We are thrilled to announce that all profits from this edition will be donated to charities. This decision reflects our deep gratitude to the community that has supported us over the years and our desire to make a meaningful impact beyond the world of investing.

We are also utterly grateful for those who played a part in making the Invest Lah project come alive. First and foremost, our heartfelt thanks go to Sean Seah and Cayden Chang for planting the seed of this book and believing in us back in 2012. To our readers, your unwavering support has been the cornerstone of our success. To the seven investors featured in this edition, thank you for enthusiastically agreeing to share your wisdom and experiences. And finally, to our family and friends, your encouragement and support have been our rock, not just through the Invest Lah journey, but in every aspect of our lives.

We hope this book inspires you, whether you are just starting your investing journey or are a seasoned investor seeking new perspectives. As we celebrate this milestone, we remain committed to empowering individuals to take charge of their financial futures — because everyone should be thinking about investing. Here's to the next decade of learning, growing, and investing together.

Happy reading, and if you haven't started investing, *invest lah*!

Ser Jing, Sudhan, and Wei Lin

Interview with Chin Hui Leong

Chin Hui Leong is the co-founder of The Smart Investor, which educates people on how to invest smartly by providing stock commentary and market coverage for Singapore and around the world. This interview was conducted on 14 July 2023.

Q: Can you share a bit of your background and how you get started with investing?

A: Investing really started as a hobby for me, something I was curious around 20 years ago.

The hobby became an obsession over time.

Part of the motivation to start investing was to create an additional source of income.

I read a book called *Multiple Streams of Income* that talked about not relying solely on your salary. Investing was the easiest option for me to pursue as a side hustle.

I was noticed by The Motley Fool and had the opportunity to contribute to their Best Buy Now (BBN) list.

I was one of around 20 people worldwide (and only one from Asia!) picking BBN stocks for Motley Fool co-founder David Gardner to consider.

These five BBN picks would go out to hundreds of thousands of people around the globe every month and was a huge responsibility.

In time, the Motley Fool in the US gave me the opportunity to become a service contributor including being a co-portfolio manager for one of the services, Motley Fool Supernova.

Eventually, I made a switch to investing as a full-time career around 2014 and joined the Motley Fool Singapore.

After the Fool left Singapore in 2019, I co-founded the Smart Investor with Joanna and David Kuo, and we've been doing that for the past four years.

Q: How would you describe your investment philosophy today?

A: My investment philosophy has evolved over time.

Today, I like to look for companies that are already doing well and try to understand the reasons for their success. I want to find companies that can continue to do what they do well and have enough runway for future growth.

I don't want to take on companies that are broken or mediocre, as I believe it's much more difficult for these companies to turn around.

Q: What have been some of the major changes in your investment philosophy over time?

A: When I first started investing, it felt like drinking from a fire hose.

The excitement of buying my first stock was overwhelming, and I was inundated with information, unsure of what was important.

I remember checking my stock price numerous times a day and worrying about why my stock wasn't performing as well as the market.

These were common thoughts: Why is my stock down 10% today? Should I sell? Did I make the right decision?

The first major epiphany for me was realising that much of the information is just noise.

For instance, one of my stocks went up 10% because the CEO rang the opening bell at NASDAQ. It seemed irrelevant to the business's fundamentals but highlighted how random stock movements can be.

The second epiphany was learning to hold stocks even when they fell between 20% and 30%.

Initially, I felt distressed when a stock's price dropped, fearing I had made a mistake.

However, I realised that if the stock was fundamentally strong — generating free cash flow and profitable — then it would likely recover over time. This realisation helped me build conviction to hold onto my stocks through downturns and even buy more when prices were low.

The most significant turning point came in 2008.

I read an article by Bill Nygren discussing Michael Steinhardt's strategy of "wiping the slate clean." This concept was crucial during the financial crisis when around 80% NASDAQ stocks fell by 50% or more.

In effect, I mentally reviewed my portfolio as if I were starting from scratch.

The process immediately exposed my mistakes like buying stocks just because their prices were falling rather than based on their fundamental strength.

What's more, Steinhardt's process revealed that I had bought more of the stocks I was less confident about and less of those I believed in strongly.

Ideally, you should allocate more to high-conviction stocks and less to those you are less confident in. But in the heat of the market crash, I was misled into buying low-conviction stocks just because their stock price was falling.

All was not lost.

The financial crisis, while challenging, clarified which companies could thrive despite adverse conditions.

Companies like Apple, Booking Holdings, and Lululemon continued to grow during the downturn, demonstrating their resilience.

This experience taught me to view the market with a fresh perspective and invest in companies that can withstand and prosper through difficult times. As Marcel Proust said, "The only real voyage of discovery consists not in seeking new landscapes, but in having new eyes."

Q: What worries you and excites you the most today?

A: What worries me the most is the potential impact of the recent pandemic-driven downturn.

Having lived through the Great Financial Crisis, which lasted about one and a half years, I recognise the emotional toll of seeing continual declines.

In 2022, we faced a similar scenario with persistent negative returns, which can feel like a prolonged period of discouragement — akin to receiving a bad report card for an extended time.

A concerning trend I've observed is how people's attitudes have shifted.

During downturns, there's a tendency for sentiment to move from intense love for stocks to a state of indifference.

As the saying goes, "The opposite of love is not hate, but indifference."

This indifference, where investors stop caring about their stocks, is troubling. It worries me that investors might be so disheartened by a challenging year that they could abandon their investment strategies and miss valuable opportunities.

Despite these concerns, there's also a significant opportunity.

The current period, while difficult, is instructive.

It's a chance to identify companies that have performed well despite the downturn and use this as a basis for future investments. In fact, I believe that the period we're in now could be one of the best times to find promising stocks for long-term growth. The key is to stay engaged, analyse the market carefully, and recognise the potential in companies that have navigated the recent challenges effectively.

What excites me the most is being able to invest alongside visionary, optimistic leaders who are trying to make the world better.

In the past decade, we've witnessed transformative developments that have profoundly impacted our lives.

Smartphones have revolutionised communication and technology, Amazon has evolved from Jeff Bezos's desk made of doors to a retail giant, and Netflix has grown from a DVD rental service to a global streaming powerhouse with almost 280 million subscribers.

Today, we're seeing incredible innovations across various fields from generative AI to genomics. For instance, there are new tests that can detect up to 50 types of cancers, some of which previously had no screening options. As we observe these groundbreaking developments, it's impossible not to feel inspired and motivated to be part of this dynamic future.

Whether or not every innovation will succeed, the enthusiasm and optimism driving these advancements are contagious. Being alongside such forward-thinking individuals and contributing to the betterment of the world is both thrilling and fulfilling.

Q: Can you share your worst investing mistake and the takeaways from that experience?

A: One of my worst mistakes was selling half of my Netflix position back in 2010 or 2011.

I tried to rationalise it by creating spreadsheets, but in reality, I was just masking my fear of losing what I had gained. Letting go of a "super stock" like Netflix too early was a huge mistake.

Another mistake was investing in Chinese companies based on a ranking system I created in a spreadsheet.

I ended up losing everything on that investment, even though I timed it almost perfectly near the bottom of the financial crisis. The key takeaway is that the quality of the company you choose matters much more than any quantitative model.

Q: What are some of the best investments you have made?

A: One standout example is Netflix.

Despite the stock being up over 100× for me, I'm cautious about calling it a great investment solely based on its returns. When I first invested, my understanding of financial metrics like free cash flow was limited.

Back then, I was primarily drawn to their DVD rental model.

Since then, Netflix has evolved into a dominant force in online streaming, showcasing how much the company has grown and transformed beyond my initial expectations.

Another notable investment is Chipotle, which I began investing in back in 2007, the same as Netflix.

At that time, the company was at the forefront of the healthy eating movement, offering tasty and nutritious food. It was my first foray into restaurant stocks, and its straightforward business model made it easy for me to grasp and appreciate.

Both of these investments were made before the Great Financial Crisis, which reinforces the idea that it's not just about when you buy, but what you buy.

The business fundamental is what truly matters in the long run.

Interview with Christopher Tan

Christopher is the founder and chief executive officer of Providend, the first fee-only wealth advisory firm in Southeast Asia. This interview was conducted on 16 May 2024.

Q: Can you share your background with our audience?

A: I completed a diploma in engineering without having any interest in it. After graduation, I decided to sign up with the army because I enjoyed it and because my family was so poor that, as the second eldest, I was asked to start working as soon as possible.

While in the army, I did a part-time degree in finance, thinking I wanted to pursue a career in finance after leaving the army. I left the army at the end of 1996, going into 1997, right smack during the Asian Financial Crisis. It was very difficult to get a job in finance then.

As a result, I spent about a year and three months with Johnson & Johnson in their pharmaceutical division. After the crisis blew over, I wanted to move into financial services.

Back in the 90s, if you wanted to do personal finance, you either joined an insurance company or a bank. I decided to join an insurance company, hoping to do financial planning.

I spent three years with the insurance company and did pretty well, earning good money. However, I wasn't doing much financial planning; it was mostly product selling. After three years, I got tired of it and quit the insurance company. In 2000, I started my own firm, Providend.

Q: What is your investment philosophy, and how has it evolved over the years?

A: Initially, I had no investment philosophy, merely following popular advice and trends. I began investing at the young age of 25, and you might be surprised by my first investment choice.

In those days, Singaporeans placed great value on the "five C's," one of which was country clubs. People believed that owning a country club was a good investment. So, my initial foray into investing was purchasing a country club for about $27,000 — quite a sum back then. Unfortunately, I didn't conduct any due diligence and ended up buying a country club with a land lease about to expire. As a result, I lost every single cent.

During the 90s, initial public offerings (IPOs) were very popular. The strategy was simple: buy lots of IPOs, hope to get a few on the listing day, sell them, and then enjoy a nice meal. I followed this approach but lost money on both IPOs and country clubs because not all IPOs performed well on their debut.

Over the years of learning from my mistakes, however, I've developed a philosophy that is aligned closely with the investment principles of my firm. This philosophy is anchored in the concept of "sufficiency," which involves understanding what is enough and finding contentment.

Contentment is not about passive acceptance or resignation but an active pursuit of what is most important to you. It requires reflection and distilling down to what truly matters, what I refer to as "non-negotiable life goals." Once you identify these goals, you should align your finances and investments to support them.

According to the philosophy of sufficiency, my investment strategy focuses on achieving "enough returns" — returns that are sufficient to meet your non-negotiable life goals while being realistic and reliable in the long term. My approach is to seek investments with a high probability of success in achieving these returns. This involves:

- Identifying asset classes supported by evidence that can provide long-term returns.
- Selecting instruments that effectively execute these asset classes.
- Staying invested and globally diversified while keeping costs as low as possible.

By adhering to these principles, we aim to achieve the highest probability of securing sufficient returns.

Q: Has the COVID-19 pandemic changed you as an investor in any way?

A: I wouldn't say that COVID-19 fundamentally changed my investment approach, but it did profoundly impact my understanding of life and, indirectly, made me a better advisor and investor.

During the past three years, COVID-19 coincided with a deeply personal period of loss and change. I lost my father, then my father-in-law a year and a half later, followed by my mother just three months later. My mother-in-law had passed away earlier, so I lost all my remaining parents within three years. To add to that, my daughter left for overseas education just a month before my mother passed away, creating a significant separation.

During the same year that my mother died and my daughter left, my wife's health took a severe downturn, and I found myself as the main caregiver. The sense of solitude and responsibility was overwhelming.

In light of these experiences, I questioned the traditional wisdom of saving and investing for the future. They say that good investors must first be good savers, focusing on delayed gratification. But I've come to realise the importance of intentional money for today.

While delayed gratification is a valid principle — saving and investing for future consumption — it's crucial to also allocate funds for the present.

This means setting aside money to build meaningful memories with loved ones while they are still with us. Investing and saving should not be solely about postponing enjoyment, but also about finding balance. The purpose of investing should be to enrich our lives and those of the people we care about.

Therefore, while COVID-19 didn't alter my investment philosophy or approach, it has refined my perspective. Now, beyond focusing on emergency funds and long-term investments, I emphasise the importance of reserving resources to enhance our present lives and relationships. This balance is key to both personal fulfilment and effective financial planning.

Q: Thank you for sharing your deeply personal story. You brought up some interesting reflections there. If you could go back in time, is there anything you would have done differently in your investing and financial planning approach?

A: People often ask me if I would change anything if I could turn back time. I typically find this question challenging because I believe there's a reason for everything we go through in life.

We cannot rewind the past, and even if we could, I'm not certain I would change anything. Our experiences shape who we are, and without them, we would be different people.

However, if pressed to answer, I would say that I wish I had learned about investing earlier — what it truly means to invest — and had embraced the philosophy of sufficiency sooner. I would have started investing earlier and applied this philosophy to set aside not just time but also money to spend meaningfully with my loved ones, especially my mother.

I often dreamed of the day when I'd be financially successful and could do wonderful things for my mom. While I have no regrets about the effort I made, including attending every medical appointment with her, there were other experiences I had hoped to share with her but delayed until I felt financially secure. Seeing friends share moments like taking their parents on trips or treating them to special experiences brings me joy, yet also a sense of missed opportunity, as my mom is no longer here to enjoy these things with me.

Ultimately, while I might wish I had made different choices in terms of time and money spent with loved ones, these experiences have contributed to who I am today. They've made me a better advisor and person. The lessons learnt and the growth that came from these experiences are invaluable, shaping my approach to both life and work.

Q: What are some of the worst investing mistakes you've made, and what did you learn from them?

A: My biggest investing mistakes were buying into country clubs and IPOs without doing proper due diligence as shared earlier. I learnt the importance of understanding what you're investing in and not just blindly following trends.

I also learnt that it's very difficult for even the best active managers to consistently beat the market, so I prefer a globally diversified portfolio of index or systematic funds with low costs.

Q: Who are your role models, and why?

A: I don't have a traditional investment role model in the way you might think, like George Soros or Howard Marks, because my approach is more about indexing and broad market exposure. But after much reflection, I've realised that my true role models are actually my mom and my wife.

Both of them embody qualities that I deeply admire and strive to emulate in my own life. They are incredibly prudent and committed to long-term financial health.

My mom, for example, was the epitome of financial prudence. She was always saving diligently, living below her means, and preparing for the future. Even though she didn't actively invest, her approach to managing her finances was a testament to her discipline.

Similarly, my wife has shown remarkable financial wisdom. When I started my business, finances were tight, and she made do with seeking out bargains and comparing prices.

Today, although our financial situation has improved, she maintains the same frugal habits. She continues to spend below her means and actively seeks out investment opportunities. She's even more proactive than I am, frequently asking me about upcoming Treasury bills and managing her own investments with keen interest.

My mom's and wife's steadfast commitment to living within their means and investing wisely has profoundly influenced me.

Interview with Dawn Cher

Dawn Cher is a leading personal finance influencer based in Singapore and runs the SG Budget Babe blog. This interview was conducted on 22 April 2024.

Q: Can you share your background with the audience?

A: I have run a financial media brand, SG Budget Babe, for over 10 years, where I cover personal finance 101 and teach people how to become savvier with their money.

Q: What was the key moment that got you started on investing?

A: There were two key moments for me. The first was when my blog unexpectedly went viral early on. I received a comment from another finance blogger who mentioned that with the $20,000 I had successfully saved, I should consider investing it rather than keeping it in the bank. I was unfamiliar with investing at the time, so that comment prompted me to dive into investment books to further understand investing, the titles of which you can find listed on my blog under a "Recommended Finance Books" article.

The second memorable moment occurred in the second or third year of running my blog. Initially, I focused on saving money, avoiding overspending, and setting aside funds for future needs. However, I quickly realized that no matter how much I saved, there was a limit to how far I could go. I understood that to truly advance, I needed to increase my income. This could be achieved through either active income from employment or side hustles, or by making money work for me through investing. This realization reinforced the importance of investing to stay ahead of inflation and secure my financial future.

Since then, I've delved deeply into investing, reading extensively the writings of Warren Buffett, Howard Marks, Charlie Munger, and Peter Lynch, among other investing greats. I've become passionate about analyzing companies, stocks, and businesses. While passive investing and ETFs are excellent foundational strategies, I find great enjoyment in stock analysis and believe it offers greater potential for capital gains. Investing should be an engaging and proactive endeavor for everyone.

Q: Can you tell us more about your investment philosophy?

A: I'm a value-growth investor who is also building up my dividend portfolio. While it might sound like I want everything, let me explain. I focus on finding undervalued companies that are also growing. I don't do deep value investing or bargain hunting where you wait for a turnaround. I prefer not to invest in companies where assets are trading below their value, waiting for the market to recognize them or for privatization to occur.

Instead, I follow the approach of Warren Buffett and Charlie Munger: looking for companies that are fairly or undervalued because the market doesn't fully understand them at present. These companies might be undervalued due to gaps in knowledge, lack of publicity, or limited coverage by analysts compared to their peers. This kind of investing excites me because it involves finding hidden value and growth potential.

At the same time, I aim to eventually retire with passive income, which is why I started with dividend investing, particularly in the Singapore market. Dividends are attractive and provide a tangible income stream, motivating investors like me.

Additionally, I invest a small portion of my portfolio in cryptocurrencies. While this is controversial and high-risk, I view certain crypto projects as undervalued with significant growth potential. For instance, I predicted back in 2017–2018 that more institutions would adopt Bitcoin, recognising its value as a digital asset. At that time, few people believed me, but look at where we are today with the U.S. Securities and Exchange Commission (SEC) approving crypto exchange-traded funds (ETFs) and even governments buying Bitcoin for their national reserves. However, I keep my crypto investments limited due to the high risks involved, treating them as an alternative asset play.

Q: Where do you find inspiration for your investment ideas?

A: When I started investing, I began by looking at the brands and companies around me. For instance, since I used a MacBook, I would research Apple. Being active on Facebook and Instagram led me to explore Meta. Initially, my focus was on the consumer (B2C) sector because these were the brands and products I was familiar with.

As I grew more experienced, I expanded my focus to the business-to-business (B2B) sector. For example, when I went for health screenings, I became interested in the companies that manufactured the machines used in these screenings. I would investigate the brands behind these machines and their suppliers, considering factors like the ageing population and the increasing demand for such equipment.

Ideas can come from various sources — sometimes from my work, news stories, or even conversations with friends. The key is developing a mindset that constantly looks for investment opportunities in everything around you.

Another source of investment ideas for me comes from subscriptions. I follow certain authors and experts who run subscription services where they share their insights and recommendations. I'm selective about which subscriptions I invest in. Typically, I'll follow a subscription for about a year, evaluating the ideas presented during that time. If I don't find at least one or two actionable insights after a year, it usually means the alignment with my investment philosophy is off, and I'll unsubscribe.

However, I sometimes continue with subscriptions even if the exact stock recommendations aren't perfect. This is because the ideas can often lead me to related companies or sectors that I might not have discovered otherwise. So, while some of these ideas come from paid sources, others emerge from free content, random conversations, or various sources of information.

Q: How has COVID-19 changed the investing landscape?

A: COVID-19 led to the rise of meme stocks and faster shifts in market sentiment due to the speed of information on social media. I now demand a higher margin of safety for stocks that are trending on social media, as valuations can become extreme. The lockdowns also sparked increased interest in investing and trading, as people sought new outlets for speculation.

Q: What worries you and excites you the most about investing today?

A: What excites me the most is the thrill of finding the next undervalued gem that the market is overlooking.

One example that I'm particularly proud of is my investment in DBS Bank. During the oil crisis and concerns about bad debts, the market was very negative on DBS, but I ran the numbers and felt confident in the company's fundamentals. I went ahead and invested, and was later validated when the CEO himself bought more shares at a higher price. DBS has since more than doubled in value, and I've generated significant capital gains and dividends from that investment.

That type of discovery and conviction in an underappreciated company is what really gets me excited about investing. It's the hunt for those hidden gems that the market is missing, and the satisfaction of being proven right when everyone else was wrong. At the same time, I'm also quite intrigued by the rise of passive investing and the potential implications it could have on the markets. I wonder whether the dominance of passive strategies could lead to future inclusion events that could disrupt the status quo. While I don't have definitive answers, it's an area that I'm closely observing and thinking deeply about.

What worries me the most is the potential for a major global event, like a war, that could make it difficult to access or liquidate my investments and disrupt my retirement plans.

Q: Who is your role model in investing?

A: My role models in investing are Warren Buffett and Charlie Munger. I admire their conviction, wisdom, and ability to remain calm and disciplined in their approach. Their wit and wisdom guide me in my life as well. I also respect Howard Marks, even though his investment philosophy is not exactly aligned with what I practice. I appreciate the way Marks writes, and there's a lot of maturity in his insights, which provide a sense of calmness and perspective.

Interview with Eugene Ng

Eugene Ng is the founder and managing director of Vision Capital Fund, a long-only global equities investment fund. This interview was conducted on 22 March 2023.

Q: Could you share with us your background?

A: I'm based in Singapore and have been investing as an individual for nearly six years — my sixth anniversary is just two days away. I primarily focus on public equities and view investing as acquiring part ownership in businesses. I call my investing approach "Vision Investing." This method involves investing in companies that align with my vision of the future, aiming to support businesses that are shaping and improving the world.

My approach is unique in that it's not just about seeking short-term gains but ensuring that the businesses I invest in are ones I would be comfortable holding for the next five, ten, or even more years. It's about finding companies that resonate with my long-term vision and are well-positioned to thrive over time.

Q: I'd like to take a step back and ask about your journey. Was there a key moment that initially got you started in investing? Additionally, was there a specific moment or experience that led you to adopt the "Vision Investing" approach?

A: A key moment that really kickstarted my investing journey was actually quite an accident. About ten years ago, on Christmas Eve, I had a serious mishap while intoxicated at a beach club. I decided to attempt a somersault into a pool, but my head hit the bottom, and I ended up breaking my neck — specifically, my C1 vertebra. The injury was so severe that doctors said there was a 99% chance I would be paralyzed in some form. I had to undergo surgery with screws implanted into my skull and wore a halo brace for four months. Remarkably, I managed to recover without paralysis, but the experience left a lasting impact on me.

After recovering, my wife encouraged me to pursue something meaningful with my life. Until then, I had been focused on enjoying life's pleasures without much financial discipline. This accident and subsequent reflection led me to think seriously about my future. I had always been strong in math and enjoyed research, so I decided to delve into investing. My initial interest in stocks was sparked during my internships, where I gained a foundational understanding of stock research.

I wanted to accelerate my learning to avoid the slow and painful process of trial and error over several years by joining a course. I quickly realised the power of value investing, particularly through companies with strong profit margins. For example, in Singapore, there's a company called Vicom that provides mandatory car inspection services. Its high-profit margin, around 30–40%, was a clear demonstration of how valuable the business could be.

Regardless of economic conditions — whether good or bad — cars still need to undergo inspections. This provides a steady revenue stream for the company. However, I noticed that the revenue growth for these kinds of companies was expected to be slow, which meant their stock prices were likely to grow at a similar low rate. This led to an aha moment for me, highlighting the limitations of investing in businesses with modest growth prospects in Singapore.

This realisation pushed me to explore investment opportunities beyond Asia, and I was amazed by what I found in the U.S. There, I discovered a wealth of faster-growing companies with larger addressable markets and more substantial growth potential. This exploration opened my mind and played a significant role in shaping my approach to Vision Investing.

One of the most profound influences on me was David Gardner from The Motley Fool. His quote, "Make your portfolio reflect your best vision of the future," deeply resonated with me. It underscored the importance of aligning investments with a forward-looking vision.

Q: It seems like your investment philosophy revolves around two key pillars: first, investing in companies that contribute positively to the world in their unique ways over the long run; and second, focusing on the idea that earnings drive stock prices over time. Is there anything else that might be an important part of your investment philosophy that we may have missed?

A: Over the long run, investing is about understanding the fundamentals. Short-term market movements often involve noise and fluctuations driven by changes in valuation multiples. However, over the long term, it's the growth in revenues, profits, and cash flows that truly drives shareholder returns.

Investing, in my view, is a game of probabilities and payoffs. Our approach is structured to maximise both the probability of success and the magnitude of potential payoffs. For example, if you hold a stock for just one day, you might have a 50% chance of making money due to the market's general upward trend. Holding a stock for a year increases this probability to about 60%. But if you hold an index for 10 to 20 years or more, the probability of a positive return rises to almost 80–90%.

Therefore, it's crucial to extend your investment horizon to increase your chances of success. We focus on finding companies with the potential for long-term growth. In reality, only about 1–2% of companies account for the majority of market returns. Many companies either generate negative returns or perform similarly to the market.

We seek out "multi-baggers" — investments that can yield returns of 5×, 10×, 20×, or even more. These are companies with high growth potential where the downside risk is limited, while the upside can be substantial. The goal is to identify opportunities with highly asymmetric payoffs, where a few successful investments generate most of the portfolio's returns.

Our criteria for selecting companies include:

- **Strong competitive advantages**: We look for businesses with enduring competitive advantages or "moats," such as pricing power and the ability to sustain profit margins.
- **High returns on capital**: We prefer companies with high or increasing rates of return on invested capital, as they can reinvest profits effectively and grow faster.
- **Large market potential**: Companies should operate in large or expanding markets to ensure long-term growth prospects.
- **Strong management**: Effective capital allocation and strong leadership are critical. We look for companies with exceptional

management teams that demonstrate a consistent ability to execute and build a strong company culture.

- **Impact and relevance**: We invest in companies that are meaningful to their customers and would be missed if they disappeared. This indicates their significance and contribution to their industry.

We generally employ a bottom-up approach, focusing on individual companies rather than market trends or sector rotations. Companies that meet our criteria undergo rigorous evaluation to ensure they are fundamentally strong and poised for long-term success.

This approach helps us shift towards higher probabilities of success and larger payoffs, ultimately guiding our investment decisions.

Q: What are the top three investing lessons that have learnt over the past couple of years?

A: The first investing lesson is the importance of thorough, independent research. Always start with primary sources. Read through company reports, earnings presentations, and other direct information rather than relying on secondary sources or analyst reports. Understanding the business drivers, such as revenue sources, profit margins, and reinvestment rates, is crucial. Evaluate customer retention and revenue stability to grasp the company's core operations.

Conduct this research over an extended period to capture trends and avoid making decisions based on short-term fluctuations. It's essential to understand what makes a business unique and evaluate its strengths thoroughly.

Once you've done your research, assess whether the company meets your investment criteria. Determine if it exhibits the traits you're looking for and consider its valuation to estimate potential returns. Always maintain your own independent conviction rather than relying on others' opinions. If someone recommends a stock and it subsequently drops, remember that the underlying business might still be sound, and the decline could present a buying opportunity rather than a reason to sell.

Maintaining a clear thesis for your investments is vital. When the market fluctuates, your original conviction should guide your decisions. If the business fundamentals remain strong, a market downturn could be an opportunity to increase your position rather than sell.

From experience, I've learned that failing to do thorough research often leads to weaker investment outcomes. Over the years, I've created comprehensive documents for each investment, ranging from 60 to 100 pages. These serve as an encyclopedia of everything I know about the company, including the investment thesis, reasons for buying or selling, and any other pertinent details.

The second key lesson is to let winners run and cut losers promptly. Allow your successful investments to grow according to your thesis. The challenge arises when a previously successful investment starts to falter. In such cases, it's important to give it time — several quarters, if needed — to see if management can address the issues or if the problems are temporary.

Sometimes, even if it seems like a business is struggling, giving it more time can be beneficial. Just like a plant that requires ongoing care to thrive, some investments need patience to recover and grow. It's important to differentiate between temporary setbacks and fundamental structural impairments.

For instance, I rarely cut positions or rotate them to other opportunities because this can often lead to mistakes. A notable example was with a company called "Arista Networks" which I initially thought was at its peak. The company faced challenges, including revenue concentration and slowing growth. Despite these issues, the position had become significant in my portfolio, so I decided to hold. Eventually, the company's performance improved as it adapted and grew its revenues, demonstrating that sometimes patience pays off.

Cutting losers is generally more straightforward. For example, if a company's revenue growth drops from 60% to 30% over several quarters, it becomes evident that the company is struggling. While cutting losers can be easier to identify, the impact on the overall portfolio is usually minimal because these positions often make up a small portion of it.

One of my biggest mistakes was an investment in a German payments company, "Wirecard AG." The company was involved in fraud and eventually failed. Despite early warnings and red flags in the *Financial Times*, my bullishness on the stock blinded me to these issues. This experience taught me the importance of not being swayed by initial enthusiasm and always staying objective.

Since then, I've adopted a more systematic approach to evaluating investments. I use a color-coding system for earnings reviews: green for good, yellow for caution, and red for bad. This objective method helps me avoid biases and make better decisions based on data rather than emotions. For example, if I see many red dots in my reviews, it signals potential issues that should not be ignored.

Despite the lessons learned, my investment in Wirecard resulted in a significant loss, which remains one of my largest. However, this experience has reinforced the importance of maintaining an unbiased perspective and carefully reviewing all data points before making decisions.

Q: If you could go back in time, what would be the one thing that you would have that you would do differently?

A: Currently, my portfolio includes slightly over 65 holdings. Interestingly, about 20 to 30 of these positions account for approximately 80–90% of the portfolio. This might seem diversified at first glance, but it's actually quite concentrated due to the strong performance of a few key positions.

Over the past couple of years, this concentration has increased. If I were to adjust my approach, I would intentionally trim down the portfolio to between 30 and 50 holdings. At its peak, my portfolio had over 80 positions, which made it very challenging to track. Many of these positions were too small and not particularly meaningful.

I've realised that being too liberal with the number of holdings can complicate portfolio management. Although I've been reducing the number of positions, the turnover has remained relatively low. For instance, last year the turnover was about 7–8%, and previously it was around 11–12%. This is still significantly lower than the turnover of many popular managers, which can exceed 60%.

Going forward, my goal is to consciously trim the portfolio down to around 15–20 core holdings. I expect that the top 20–30 positions should account for the majority of the portfolio. This adjustment will help maintain focus and ensure that the core positions drive the majority of the portfolio's performance. Lowering the number of holdings should improve overall management and reduce the need for frequent adjustments.

Q: What has been your best investment to date?

A: The biggest investment I've made to date has been in Trade Desk. It has been a significant winner, increasing my original capital by about three to five times. The growth of Trade Desk has been tremendous.

When we first examined Trade Desk, we saw it operating in the programmatic advertising space. In digital advertising, you typically think of search advertising, like Google, and social media advertising, such as Facebook or Instagram. Programmatic advertising, where Trade Desk excels, operates outside of these major platforms.

Programmatic advertising allows advertisers to purchase ad space through various platforms rather than directly on platforms like Google or Facebook. Trade Desk operates on the buy side, helping advertisers manage and optimise their ad spending. This gives Trade Desk a strong position with higher margins and pricing power compared to sell-side platforms, which have less control over pricing.

The company's founder, Jeff Green, has a deep understanding of the market and has been able to execute a clear strategy effectively. Trade Desk started with display advertising and has since moved into connected TV (CTV), finding a successful niche in each area.

Trade Desk's consistent performance is notable. It has shown revenue growth rates of over 20% each quarter for the past three to five years. This durable growth, combined with strong profitability, has contributed significantly to the portfolio's performance.

Initially, Trade Desk was valued at a premium due to its fast growth and profitability. However, this premium valuation was justified, and the returns have proven attractive. The company's ability to maintain high growth and profitability highlights its strong position in the market.

Q: Who is your role model in life?

A: I'm still in the process of discovering my ultimate role model. However, David Gardner has been a very influential figure for me, particularly because of his philosophical approach to investing. His perspective on stock selection has been impactful.

When I think about role models in investing, I ask myself, "If I weren't doing this, where would I put my money?" For me, the answer would be to invest with someone who demonstrates consistency and high integrity.

Consistency is crucial in investing. Many people may speak well, but their actions often don't align with their words. Over time, I've realised that very few people exhibit true consistency while maintaining high integrity and responsibility toward their investment theses. Those who manage to stay independent and true to their principles are extremely rare.

I've encountered many successful investors, but not all of them can sustain high returns over the long term. Some investors who are already quite old may not have the consistency needed to continue achieving high returns. I'm still learning and trying to identify such role models.

Interview with Royston Yang

Royston Yang is a portfolio manager at The Smart Investor, which educates people on how to invest smartly by providing stock commentary and market coverage for Singapore and around the world. This interview was conducted on 16 January 2024.

Q: Could you share your background with the audience?

A: I graduated from NTU with a Bachelor of Accountancy in 2000. After that, I worked in audit for about two years. Following my time in audit, I transitioned to corporate accounting, which is a common path for auditors. I spent nearly a decade in corporate accounting.

Next, I moved to a hedge fund, focusing on investment and financial modelling. I worked in the investment industry for approximately six years before transitioning to my current role as a portfolio manager and writer for The Smart Investor. I also write freelance for the Motley Fool USA.

Q: What was that key moment that got you into investing?

A: My journey into investing began in my 20s. I started by having a conversation with my dad. I asked him if he invested his money, and he mentioned that he was investing in some Singapore stocks. Curious about how I could grow my own money, I asked him for more details. He provided a brief introduction to investing, and from there, I took the initiative to read and learn more on my own.

Q: How would you summarise your investment philosophy in a couple of sentences?

A: My investment philosophy centres on value investing, where I focus on great companies that have the potential for long-term growth.

I adopt a very long-term approach, meaning that once I buy something, I usually don't sell it unless something goes wrong. My holding period is often 10 years or more. As long as the business's story remains strong, I will continue to hold the investment. My longest-held investment has been for two decades.

Q: Where do you get your investment ideas from?

A: I source my investment ideas from two main places. First, I read a variety of business articles from sources like The Business Times, Wall Street Journal, and Bloomberg.

Second, I discuss ideas with investor friends who share my philosophy, exposing myself to different perspectives. These are my primary sources for generating investment ideas.

Q: How has COVID-19 changed you as an investor?

A: That's an interesting question. COVID-19 was truly unexpected, and no one had seen anything like it before, even in terms of investment. It taught me that unforeseen events can occur suddenly and drastically. This underscores the importance of having a robust investment philosophy. Additionally, we've seen that many growth stocks that thrived during COVID-19 have not performed well afterwards. This indicates that trends may not last forever.

Q: What worries you when it comes to investing?

A: What worries me most is the possibility of missing out on something critical for my investments. When I develop an investment thesis, I strive to cover all bases and account for all risks.

My primary concern is encountering an unforeseen risk or facing results worse than anticipated. For example, if I expect poor results but the outcomes turn out to be disastrous, I would need to revisit my investment thesis and possibly sell the stock if it no longer aligns with my expectations.

Q: On the flip side, looking forward to the next couple of years, what excites you the most?

A: What excites me is the potential for the businesses I invest in to continue growing and innovating. Human ingenuity drives progress, whether in technology, medicine, robotics, or other fields, and being an investor allows me to witness and be part of this advancement. I find it thrilling to have a front-row seat to watch these developments unfold and grow alongside the companies I own.

Q: If you could turn back time, what is that one thing that you would have done differently?

A: One of my main regrets is not investing in real estate investment trusts (REITs) earlier. Instead, I experimented with small-cap stocks that had high dividend yields, but they didn't perform well, and I ended up selling them. If I had invested in REITs sooner, I would have accumulated a substantial amount of dividend income by now. As it stands, I'm starting this investment strategy later than I would have liked.

Q: Could you share some of your investing mistakes and the key takeaways you've learned from them?

A: Some of my investing mistakes include buying companies with excessive debt. I didn't fully appreciate how punishing debt can be, especially when conditions deteriorate. I invested in companies that were heavily leveraged to fuel rapid growth, but when things went wrong, they faced significant problems due to their high debt levels.

Another mistake was investing in companies with unusually high dividend yields, often exceeding 10%. I thought these yields were sustainable, but the businesses eventually faltered and some even went bankrupt. Fortunately, I managed to sell before they collapsed, but this experience taught me the importance of avoiding unsustainable dividend yields.

Q: The best investment to date?

A: Without a doubt, my best investment has been in iFAST. Since I invested in 2017, its value has increased approximately 11 times.

Q: What are some books that have shaped your life?

A: *The Intelligent Investor* by Benjamin Graham is a foundational book for value investors. Additionally, Howard Marks' *The Most Important Thing* has been crucial for me. It has taught me to think about market cycles, second-level thinking, and to look beyond the obvious. These two resources have been pivotal in my investment journey.

Q: If you could give three pieces of advice to a beginner investor, what would they be?

A: First would be to accept market volatility: Volatility is a normal part of investing. Share prices can fluctuate widely due to human emotions and market dynamics. Understanding that these fluctuations are normal can help you stay calm and make more informed decisions.

Second is to invest for the long term. Focus on the long-term potential of your investments rather than short-term market movements. While short-term market activity can be unpredictable, a solid, long-term investment strategy will generally lead to positive outcomes if the underlying business performs well.

Last but not least, expect to make mistakes as mistakes are an inevitable part of investing. Even experienced investors like Warren Buffett make them. The key is to learn from your mistakes and make adjustments to your strategy to improve over time.

Q: Who's your role model?

A: Warren Buffett's approach to investing and living has always been an inspiration to me. It's remarkable how someone can be extremely wealthy yet maintain such a frugal lifestyle.

His ability to balance immense success with modest living is a testament to his values and discipline. This contrast is particularly striking given the pressures and expectations that often come with wealth.

Buffett's example shows that true success isn't just about accumulating wealth, but also about how you manage it and live your life. His approach offers valuable lessons for everyone.

Interview with Thomas Chua

Thomas Chua runs the Steady Compounding website, providing investing research for the public. This interview was conducted on 18 February 2023.

Q: Please share with us your background and also like what you're doing right now.

A: I was formerly from the civil service in Singapore because I took on a bonded scholarship to alleviate my family's financial pressures. But when I signed the scholarship contract, I knew I would eventually quit. Because I've known early on that my passion was in investing, so once I've earned the privilege of pursuing my passion, I would make a pivot.

As my bond was ending, I began writing on online platforms with the intention of finding a career in investments. However, my writing gained traction and connected me with other investors. Through these interactions, I realised I could pursue investing full-time and achieve the growth I wanted by exchanging ideas with fellow investors.

Currently, I write full-time at https://steadycompounding.com/, where I share my investment research and insights with readers.

Q: Rolling back time for a moment, do you remember when you first started investing? What was the trigger or inspiration behind buying your first stock?

A: I was 17 years old back then, and I remember it vividly. A friend of mine passed me the book *Rich Dad Poor Dad*. He told me that one of his mentors gave it to him and insisted he read it, but he never did, so he passed it on to me. When I read it, I was quite mind-blown because it felt like the book spoke directly to me. The way it described the mindset of a "poor dad" versus a "rich dad" resonated with my own family situation and highlighted what we were lacking.

The book showed me a new way of thinking, which I wouldn't have considered otherwise. While it wasn't a great "how-to" book, it was an excellent "why" book. It gave me a compelling reason to start investing. That was when I started diving deep into everything I could find about investing in the library. I explored a wide spectrum of topics, including technical analysis. Eventually, I settled on quality compounding, which is where I am now.

The first stock I bought was Cambridge Industrial Trust. I didn't know much about the company, but after hearing my aunt talk about it, I decided to invest $2,000 in it. Fortunately, I didn't lose money, though I didn't make much either. But I clearly remember that it was the first company I ever bought shares in.

Q: You mentioned quality compounding. Maybe could you share with us what's your investment philosophy?

A: I look for companies with a moat and that are still expanding. They should also still have opportunities to reinvest at very high returns.

Q: Where do you get your investment ideas from?

A: There are a few places where I get ideas. First, I'm very active on X (formerly Twitter), where many people share ideas with me. It helps to be part of a group of investors who always share ideas and play devil's advocate for each other. Another place I like to fish for ideas is the 13F filings. These filings require big fund managers to declare their positions every quarter. I use them to hunt for companies that fall within my circle of competence and align with my investment philosophy.

Q: How about websites or blogs?

A: When it comes to company breakdowns, Ser Jing's The Good Investors (https://www.thegoodinvestors.sg/) and Chin Hui Leong's The Smart Investors (https://thesmartinvestor.com.sg/) are both excellent websites. There are a few others like Motley Fool and Seeking Alpha, which publishes a large volume of content.

What I like to do is post about a company on X. Once I do, people start sharing resources from many different places. Another website I highly recommend is Saber Capital, run by John Huber — it's excellent.

Additionally, although not specifically for investing, Morgan Housel's writings are very good for developing a mindset towards investing, even if they don't focus on specific companies.

Q: How has the COVID-19 pandemic changed you as an investor?

A: I think one thing Covid has changed is the perception of the phrase "this time is different." Usually, it's not so different. Back then, the buzz was around hyper-growth companies, but risks often materialise when people least expect them. For the longest time, interest rates were extremely low until last year, when they started hiking aggressively. We need to be cautious about valuations because the romantic story back then was that internet companies could grow at a high rate for a very long time.

Almost all the investors I know were caught up in the idea that these companies would grow to eventually justify their valuations. However, as we've seen in recent quarterly results, many of these companies have been significantly affected by the economic slowdown. The biggest lesson is that it is seldom truly different. Although the companies now are much better than those during the dot-com bubble, we still have to be very mindful about their valuations.

During the dot-com bubble, many companies didn't even generate revenue but still commanded extremely high valuations. For example, Cloudflare was at one point trading at 100 times price-to-sales. They are a revenue-generating company with clear operating leverage, but the price tag was still too steep to stomach. So, while the companies today may be better, the valuation concerns remain significant.

Q: Looking ahead to the next 10 years, what trends, innovations, or developments do you find particularly exciting?

A: I think a lot about innovation, and I always like to refer to a Warren Buffett or Charlie Munger quote. They suggest that when it comes to technology, it doesn't necessarily differentiate a company in the long run. For example, when escalators were first introduced, the retailers who installed them in their shopping malls had an initial advantage, but eventually, everyone else adopted them too.

When choosing investments, I consider technology beneficial but ask myself what prevents competitors from using it. Many of these SaaS (software-as-a-service) companies are excellent, but technology alone doesn't provide a lasting competitive advantage. I always go back to thinking about more traditional moats, such as network effects, branding, and other barriers to entry.

So, while I'm aware of the latest developments, I focus on understanding the fundamental economic moats that sustain a company's advantage over time.

Q: Looking back over the past 10 years, if you could condense the top three investing lessons you've learned, what would they be?

A: Looking back over the past 10 years, I've learned several key investing lessons:

- **Transitioning from deep value to quality investing**: I took a long time to shift from focusing on dividend and deep value investing to investing in quality companies. Initially, I invested in companies trading below net cash, such as Creative Technologies and Cosco (the shipping company and not the U.S. retailer). Although these companies seemed safe, the opportunity cost was significant. Quality growth companies often present better growth prospects. I wish I had transitioned to evaluating companies based on their overall quality and growth potential sooner, rather than just focusing on the balance sheet.
- **Understanding unprofitable companies**: I realized that many unprofitable companies, especially in their early years, should be assessed differently. For instance, companies like Amazon were unprofitable at first but invested heavily in intangibles. From an economic standpoint, their spending made sense and was aimed at long-term growth. While these companies may appear unprofitable in the short run, their unique economics and long-term potential can justify their strategies. I wish I had recognised this earlier and applied a different lens to such investments.
- **Evaluating earnings beyond dividends**: Early in my investing journey, I focused heavily on dividend-paying companies and used dividends as a primary valuation metric. However, I've learned that a company's earnings can be used in multiple ways: reinvested in the business, paid out as dividends, or used for share buybacks. It's

important to consider all these aspects rather than focusing solely on dividends. This broader perspective provides a more comprehensive understanding of a company's value and strategy.

These lessons have been crucial in refining my investing approach and improving my overall strategy.

Q: What has been your best investment so far and what's your thought process behind making that investment?

A: I think the investment that prompted my transition from deep value to quality investing was Starbucks. I held Starbucks for about eight or nine years and it was the first time I bought a stock that looked expensive, with a price-to-earnings ratio above 20.

Despite its higher valuation, I ended up making more money from Starbucks than from my deep-value stocks. Although it may not seem like a very exciting choice, Starbucks was pivotal in reshaping my investment thinking. Even after this experience, it took me some time to fully adopt this new investing style, but Starbucks was the turning point.

Q: In terms of position sizing, could you share how many positions you typically hold in your portfolio at any given time?

A: I typically hold between 15 to a maximum of 25 positions in my portfolio. I follow a strategy inspired by Joel Greenblatt, who emphasizes a research-based approach to diversification. According to his research, the benefits of diversification diminish as the number of stocks increases.

For me, keeping the number of positions around 20 strikes the right balance. Having too many positions can make it challenging to understand each company thoroughly. On the other hand, holding too few positions can be risky. I've seen investors with as few as three or four positions, which can lead to significant losses if things go wrong. I prefer not to be overly concentrated, so I ensure I hold at least 15 positions at all times.

Q: When deciding to add a new stock to your portfolio, how do you determine the best way to enter the new position?

A: I usually buy new positions in tranches, typically in increments of 15%. This approach allows me to learn more about the company over time and adjust my position as I gain more insights. I find that when I first discover a potential opportunity, it's easy to get excited and overlook some risks. By buying in stages, I mitigate the risk of making a hasty decision.

For example, I'll gradually build up to a full position by buying in phases. On the other hand, if a company shows clear warning signs or fundamental issues, I may decide to sell it entirely. But generally, I prefer to invest gradually and make adjustments as I learn more.

Q: Is there a particular book or resource that has significantly shaped your investing career? If so, what is it?

A: The books that have significantly shaped my investing career are, of course, *One Up On Wall Street* by Peter Lynch and *The Joys of Compounding* by Gautam Baid. Both are excellent resources. Additionally, *100 Baggers* by Chris Mayer is another outstanding book that I would recommend.

Q: If you could give advice to a beginner investor — imagine you're speaking to your younger self at 18 — what would you say?

A: If I were to give advice to a beginner investor, especially someone just starting at 18, I would definitely recommend reading Warren Buffett's letters to shareholders and the book *The Essays of Warren Buffett.*

The annual letters can be a bit overwhelming on first read, but *The Essays of Warren Buffett* is organised by topic — such as share buybacks, return on invested capital, and management — which makes the wisdom more accessible. Reading these materials offers great insights and can be incredibly valuable.

Initially, you'll gain a lot of benefit from the first read, but as you gain more experience, revisiting these writings will provide even deeper insights, as you'll be reading with a better understanding of investing concepts. So, make it a priority to dive into Warren Buffett's letters — they're a treasure trove of knowledge.

Q: Who's your like role model in life?

A: It would definitely be Warren Buffett. I also like Charlie Munger — I agree with a lot of what he says. Two pieces of advice stand out to me. One is never feel sorry for yourself. Despite facing significant challenges — losing his son, his wife leaving him, losing an eye — he never complained. He believed that the energy spent feeling sorry for oneself is better directed towards improving one's situation. This aligns with my own approach, which is to maintain a strong internal locus of control. Focus on changing what you can control and make the best out of your circumstances.

Next is to avoid envy. He emphasises that envy can destroy business and personal relationships. Many people, despite their own success, suffer because they envy others who are richer or more successful. Instead of enjoying what you have, envy leads to unnecessary dissatisfaction. His insights, including his recent observations, are filled with profound truths about maintaining a healthy perspective on life and success.

Interview with Wan Hsin Hun

Wan Hsin Hun is a full-time stock market investor and this interview was conducted on 18 February 2023.

Q: What is your background?

A: I'm a Singaporean full-time equity investor. I have been doing this for 14 years. Before that, I was a political analyst followed by being a business journalist.

Q: What was that key moment that got you started on investing?

A: After I discovered that equities can offer not only far better returns than bank deposits, but also passive income.

Q: If you could summarise your investment philosophy into a few simple sentences, what would it be?

A: I try to collect good assets. In this case, the shares of good companies which I think I would like to keep. Those are probably quality companies that offer decent yields and companies that I think I can rely on for retirement.

Q: On average, how long do you hold your stocks?

A: Usually less than three years for the outright disappointing ones. As for some long-held ones, I've been holding them since the start of my investing career. And I still don't see any good reason to sell them.

Q: How often do you reevaluate whether to continue holding or sell or buy more of the shares?

A: There's a large part of my portfolio that I do not consider selling and a smaller part that I may unload once in a long while to reinvest the proceeds or accept company buyouts. Generally, I buy to keep and most of the time I'm slowly buying.

Q: Where are some sources where you get your investment ideas?

A: The media, fellow investors, and bourse filings. There are only so many listed companies. So after studying them for so long, I roughly know which are the good or subpar ones. Sometimes these sources alert me to new developments that may change the attractiveness of these companies.

Q: How has the COVID-19 pandemic changed your view of investing?

A: To be frank, it didn't change my investing views, work habits, or lifestyle. I started out during the Global Financial Crisis, a major crisis. And I have gone through many smaller but significant market crises before the COVID-19 pandemic, another major one. So I'm not worried about stocks plunging. In fact, I'm very happy to grab rare bargains in a market panic.

Q: Are there any key lessons or memorable experiences that you would wish to share with the audience or your younger self?

A: Avoid value traps. Sometimes they may be cheap, but they may be cheap for a reason. If we find that the market prices a stock at a low valuation, ask ourselves why, especially if it's a normalised market, free from shocking news that would spook investors.

Q: Can you give one example of a value trap that initially looked attractive, but in hindsight you realised was a trap?

A: A property company that looked cheap on discount to net asset value but traded at that valuation for many years and paid little dividends. This is common among property firms due to lumpy earnings, a lack of recurring income, high capital expenditure needs, high debt, and the long cycle of real estate. And sometimes management won't unlock value or will rather reinvest most earnings for growth than pay out more. So such stocks can be a trap with the allure of looking cheap and being backed by the safety of hard assets. Their returns might be low for many years, particularly if their recurring income and payout is poor.

Q: Can you share a little as to why you generally go for companies that pay dividends?

A: Dividends are extremely important. They actually constitute part of our total returns. They give us a chance to reinvest without selling anything. It's also a way to recoup our outlay in the stock. Management can say what they want, but the dividend is one way to gauge their cash flow, business confidence and resilience, and profit-sharing consistency and intentions. And if they're able to grow the dividends, that's even better, because the increase will both lift the stock price and provide a higher dividend income.

If I may add, a dividend stock tends to put a floor under its price, with price support coming from investors chasing its dividend yield. So in a crash, it's unlikely to drop too low because the stock will trade at a higher yield on its lower price, making it even more attractive to investors.

Q: Could you share one of your best investments in the past 14 years?

A: One would be Micro-Mechanics. I first bought it in 2009 and have held it ever since — the last time I added it was in 2012.

My total returns have been 10 to 15 fold. In terms of yield on cost, it's largely 25–35%, extraordinarily high because I accumulated it at very low prices and it kept increasing dividends over the years. And importantly, I held on to the stock for a very long time.

Q: Could you share a little bit about your position sizing approach?

A: I don't have a fixed number of stocks to hold or set how much each should take up in my portfolio. But I generally don't allow any stock holding to exceed one-third of my entire portfolio. Most of my portfolio is made up of my top 15 or 20 stocks, and I hold about 40.

Q: When you want to enter a new stock, do you allocate a specific percentage of your portfolio, or do you just buy a bit and see?

A: Generally, I'll buy a bit, wait and see, buy some more, wait and see, and slowly build my position over time.

I used to buy more at the outset. But over time, I've learned to buy gradually to keep more dry powder and take time to further understand the company and its people. Spreading the purchases out also means there's a chance that the stock may dip and I could buy it cheaper.

Q: Taking a small step back from the investment-related questions, how do you think your journey as an investor has impacted you?

A: Equity investing has changed my life. It has given me income, financial security, a different lifestyle, and allowed me to know many other investors. It also enabled me to help my family to invest and has given us an exciting conversation topic and a fun, rewarding purpose. Investing isn't just about making money, it's about increasing our knowledge in different subject areas. We learn about business, people, world events and their investment impact. It has also freed up my time from salaried employment.

Q: If you could give a piece of advice to a beginner investor, what would you say?

A: Be prepared. Everyone has to put in time for homework to do well in any field. Anybody can invest money, but not that many people are willing to invest the time to back up that money. So make time to make good money. And the young investor can always seek mentors and mix with those who are also interested in investing.

There's also so much investment literature online and in print for anyone to read now. But know that while a sharp investor can outrun a careful saver, a careful saver will beat a reckless investor.

Successful, lifelong investors have at least seven traits: they read voraciously, are highly disciplined with money, think and act long-term, know their risk, tend to shun dubious opportunities, can be contrarians, and can read people reasonably well. Also know that to enjoy lasting wealth, avoid poor money choices, not just invest.

Acknowledgements

Ser Jing: I have a few groups of people I would like to thank — so bear with me for a little while! The first would of course be my family. My dad, mom, younger brother and younger sister have given me a real *home* (not just a house) to live in and for that, I am blessed. My huge extended family on both sides and the close ties we share make me proud to call them family too.

Next up, I want to thank my whole gang of friends spanning my secondary school days, my junior college years, my army and navy daze (days) and my university life — you guys have helped shaped me in many ways, both good *and bad*. But no matter what, I wouldn't want it any other way. Here's to you folks:

> The bunch from River Valley High School, you know who you are — those crazy years playing football, getting chased out of school camps and overseas escapades are still fondly remembered. May many new memories with you guys come down the years ahead.
>
> My classmates from National Junior College, remember football and DOTA? Those were awesome times… and we are still playing DOTA!
>
> I made one great friend from my National Service daze playing the guitar together and I'm glad we're still doing so to this day.
>
> University was fun because of the Engineering Science Programme folks I met in the National University of Singapore. Barbecues, chalets,

DOTA and Blackshot are what I remember from those great times (I'm tossing all the presentations and research projects away from my memory now!).

A big "Thank You!" has to go out to Cayden Chang and Sean Seah of the Mind Kinesis Value Investing Academy for approaching me and my co-authors about the idea of writing a book catered to retail investors. Without them, this book might never have happened.

I would also like to offer my heartfelt appreciation for the Motley Fool Blogging Network team who helped me hone my writing skills when I first started writing for them. Then, came the Motley Fool Singapore team — Bruce Jackson, David Kuo, Joanna Sng — whom I'll be eternally grateful to for giving me the chance to embark on a career related to investing, which I have so much passion for.

Ahh yes! How can I forget my investing buddies and co-authors, Sudhan and Weilin? You guys taught me a lot more about investing than I ever could learn by myself and it has been a privilege working together. To many more good years ahead (with beer, of course!).

Appreciation will have to go out to all the investing masters, legends and professionals who have shared their thoughts through their writings and interviews. They have allowed me to learn *so much* from their past experiences and it's my little dream that I can do the same for you, our dear reader. The Motley Fool deserves special praise as well, for building the greatest investment community in the world.

And to everyone else who has walked into my life in one way or another, thank you. Life does work in mysterious ways.

Cheers!

Sudhan: I would like to thank Sean and Cayden for believing in me and roping me in to write a book with two other gentlemen, Ser Jing and

Wei Lin. Without them, this book would not have been possible. Sean was the one who introduced me to Ser Jing and Wei Lin in September 2012 during a conference and we have clicked ever since. When we met, who would have thought we would become good friends and then go on to be co-authors, writing a book that we are extremely passionate about — investing.

Thank you to Ser Jing and Wei Lin for being such great co-authors and friends. I have learnt lots from you guys ever since we met. There are many more great things to come, I believe. To infinity and beyond, buddies!

Thank you to all my dear friends — from Outram Secondary School, Catholic Junior College, National Service, Air Transport Training College and to others who are not from the circles mentioned — whom have all given me awesome advice on the book on how to tailor it for beginners.

Thank you to all my investing friends who have crossed my life. You have helped me in one way or another to craft my investment thesis, and I am still learning from you wonderful individuals.

I am grateful to The Motley Fool Singapore team, especially to David Kuo and Joanna Sng, for helping me further my passion for writing on investing.

Thank you to Adam Khoo for unlocking the world of value investing to me, back in March 2009. Thank you to the investing giants like Benjamin Graham, Warren Buffett, Phil Fisher, Peter Lynch and many more who have selflessly shared their knowledge about investing with me through their books and speeches.

And most importantly, my deepest gratitude goes to my parents for showering me with unconditional love and to my lovely wife and kids, thank you for your unwavering support.

Wei Lin: I would like to thank the following people, without whom, this book will not be possible.

Firstly, Sean and Cayden, for giving us this opportunity to share our views on investing with our readers. As they say, a journey of a thousand miles begins with a first step and it is our honour to have taken our baby steps together with you. Sean, I will not forget our chat at TCC, NTUC building. The coffee aroma seemed distant when compared to the intensity of thoughts which flowed through our minds. Cayden, I am grateful for your openness and thoughtfulness. Regardless of your busy schedule, you still remembered the size of our shirts and listened to the ideas we bring to the table. That meant a lot to me.

Next, I would like to thank my Professor, Dr Koh Noi Keng, Chairperson of Citi-NIE Financial Literacy Hub for Teachers, for her guidance and encouragement all these years. Your passion for financial literacy and education has changed the lives of countless individuals, myself included. From the day we signed the MOU at Millenia Walk, I knew the landscape of financial literacy in Singapore would never be the same again.

I would also like to thank my Dean, Professor Ling San, Dean of College of Science, Nanyang Technological University for your continuous support in my countless endeavours. Your gems of wisdom have been my guiding light throughout these years. If time could stop for a moment or two, I wished it did when we chatted about mathematics, education, life and beyond. I promised I'll be back for tea, and if you're reading this, I would have fulfilled that promise.

To my co-authors, Ser Jing and Sudhan, as Charlie Brown once said, "In life, it's not where you go — it's who you travel with." This investing journey has been so much fun with you guys on board, I thoroughly enjoyed every single moment thus far, from the books to the booze. Ser Jing, your eye for detail never fails to amaze me and I can't get enough of your candid way of writing. Sudhan, thank you for inviting me to do the interview on your blog, I felt really honoured and it is perhaps one of the most important reflections I've ever done in my life.

To Ivan, our friendly neighbourhood business hunter, your humbleness and willingness to reinvent yourself is truly inspirational. Cheers to many more years of friendship, from Melbourne to Singapore. I have several groups of friends to thank, without whom, my life would not be so vibrant and enriching.

My investing buddies, Calvin, Chongxian, Chin Leng and Tin Man, for teaching me lessons that go way beyond money, indeed, the best things in life are free. Cheers to our dreams, friendship and everlasting happiness! Special thanks to the Singapore Outreach team at the NTU Investment Club for keeping the flame of financial literacy for youths burning strong.

To my friends, Nick, Yong, Zack, Alfie, Alan, Daryl, Ying Liang, Ching Tse, Darrell, Tian Hao, Stanley, Sydney, Andeed, Wen Quan, Chin, Hsin Hun, Royston, Aloy, Keqi, Eva and Wenhan, Joyce and Tat Leong, Milo and Jade. Thank you for all the beautiful memories thus far and cheers to many more ahead!

To the greatest teachers in the world, Zongjin, Cheryl, Hai Bee, Li Xuan, Sophia, Ivy, Zhong Shun, Darren, Sun Yu, Raavee, Nurul, Jimmy, Jason, Alvin, HOD Yong Han, Leo Mama, Rendy, Timothy, Alan Pavlov, Samuel, Guo Liang my man, Audrey BFF, Sophia, Sherry, Kenneth, Kian Chye, Wicky, Benson, Wei Wei, Chee Hsiang, Suyan, Sam, Rommel, Lynn, Sangeetha and Kelsie. Go on and inspire the world, be the change, our nation depends on you.

To my dearest SPMS YEP teammates, Gim Yean, Ming Yao, Theresa and Jiahe, Qin You, Jasper, JK, Yili, Ricky, Yu Fang, Kelvin, Zhi Yuan, Yenni, Jasmine, Liting and Don, Xiao Yu, Eugene and Jean. I have never met people whose hearts are as big and wide as yours.

To my team at HCHAIN, my partners Alan, Arthur, Ron, Eve, Ben, Clarissa and our wonderful team Penny, Kuei Yeh, Kai Ni, Lewis, Hui Ting, Celine, Ryan, Wen Han. Thank you for always making our customers' day so brew-tiful and I look forward to many more team bonding sessions to come.

To my JoyfulPerson team, Winnie, Darrell, Palash, Nic, Bao, Eliza, Giogio, Celia, Izz, Wayne, Yanzhen, Amanda, Nicole, Vaishnav, Wayne, Celest and Holly. Thank you for being on this startup journey, it certainly wasn't for the faint hearted.

Most importantly, I want to thank my family, for being with me every step of the way. I am eternally grateful for the lessons on values, courage and character. Thank you Shan Bin, Yi Ting, Shao Wee, Jing Kai, Allie, Mum and Dad for being my pillar of support and strength. This book is dedicated to each and every one of you.

XYZ Corporation's Fictional Financial Statements

Income Statement, $'000	2008	2009	2010	2011	2012
Sales Revenue	10,000	12,000	13,800	17,000	20,485
Cost of Sales	5,000	5,500	6,200	7,200	9,200
Gross Profit	**5,000**	**6,500**	**7,600**	**9,800**	**11,285**
Selling, General and Admin Expenses	2,500	2,700	3,200	3,800	3,950
Depreciation and Amortisation	1,200	1,100	950	1,150	930
Operating Earnings	**1,300**	**2,700**	**3,450**	**4,850**	**6,405**
Interest Expense	0	0	0	0	0
Income Tax Expenses	390	810	1,035	1,455	1,922
Net Income	**910**	**1,890**	**2,415**	**3,395**	**4,484**
Average No. of Diluted Shares Outstanding	10,000	10,000	10,000	10,000	10,000
Earnings Per Share	0.091	0.189	0.242	0.3395	0.448

Balance Sheet, $'000	2008	2009	2010	2011	2012
Assets					
Current Assets					
Cash & Equivalents	3,000	4,060	4,255	4,780	5,984
Accounts Receivable	2,500	3,100	4,000	3,900	4,670
Inventory	1,000	900	1,200	1,300	1,650
Prepaid Expenses	500	650	450	700	680
Non-Current Assets					
Property, Plant and Equipment (net of accumulated Depreciation)	10,000	10,100	10,250	11,600	12,970

Intangible Assets and Goodwill	5,000	5,000	6,000	7,200	7,200
Total Assets	**22,000**	**23,810**	**26,155**	**29,480**	**33,154**
Liabilities					
Current Liabilities					
Accounts Payable	1,100	1,050	1,200	1,400	1,350
Accrued Expenses Payable	300	550	700	1,000	1,200
Income Tax Payable	200	220	300	430	670
Short-term Debt and Current Portion of Long-Term Debt	0	0	0	0	0
Non-Current Liabilties					
Long-Term Debt	0	0	0	0	0
Total Liabilites	**1,600**	**1,820**	**2,200**	**2,830**	**3,220**
Equity					
Share Capital	10,000	10,000	10,000	10,000	10,000
Retained Earnings	10,400	11,990	13,955	16,650	19,934
Total Shareholders Equity	**20,400**	**21,990**	**23,955**	**26,650**	**29,934**
Cash Flow Statement, $'000	**2008**	**2009**	**2010**	**2011**	**2012**
Net Income	910	1,890	2,415	3,395	4,484
Decrease (Increase) in Accounts Receivable	–500	–600	–900	100	–770
Decrease (Increase) in Inventory	–200	100	–300	–100	–350
Decrease(Increase) in Prepaid Expenses	100	–150	200	–250	20
Increase (Decrease) in Accounts Payable	300	–50	150	200	–50
Increase (Decrease) in Accrued Expenses Payable	50	250	150	300	200
Increase (Decrease) in Income Tax Payable	30	20	80	130	240
Depreciation and Amortisation	1,200	1,100	950	1,150	930
Cash Flow From Operating Activities	**1,890**	**2,560**	**2,745**	**4,925**	**4,704**

Purchase of Property, Plant and Equipment	-900	-1,200	-1,100	-2,500	-2,300
Purchase of Intangible Assets	-100	0	-1,000	-1,200	0
Cash Flow From Investing Activities	**-1,000**	**-1,200**	**-2,100**	**-3,700**	**-2,300**
Proceeds from Short-Term Debt	0	0	0	0	0
Proceeds from Long-Term Debt	0	0	0	0	0
Cash Dividends Paid	-200	-300	-450	-700	-1200
Issuance of Stock	0	0	0	0	0
Cash Flow From Financing Activities	**-200**	**-300**	**-450**	**-700**	**-1,200**
Total Increase (Decrease) in Cash	**690**	**1,060**	**195**	**525**	**1,204**
Cash Balance at Start of the Year	**2,310**	**3,000**	**4,060**	**4,255**	**4,780**
Cash Balance at End of the Year	**3,000**	**4,060**	**4,255**	**4,780**	**5,984**

How We Started

Ser Jing: I was 18 when I first came across Philip Fisher's *Common Stocks and Uncommon Profits* — my first proper introduction to the world of investing. I was attending junior college at that time and had taken Economics as one of my four mandatory subjects. After my first month or so in junior college, I began to question the assumptions and general teachings of Economics. For example, I was told that people with too much money to spare would put all their money into bonds... Really? This irked me and I began my quest to search for and learn about people who really "understood" money and how it worked. At the same time, I had a disdain for the ferocious over-activity and hubris that surrounded this activity known as trading. My parents had some experience with the stock market, but I sometimes wondered what those tickers actually meant. Surely something real existed behind those red and green numbers? My natural leanings eventually led me to none other than the Oracle of Omaha, Warren Buffett, who counseled that there was a business behind every stock-symbol. I was hungry to find out more about his thoughts on investing and who his teachers were. It turned out that the most famous mentor Buffett had was the great Benjamin Graham and he had actually written a book called *The Intelligent Investor*. I wanted to purchase it but when I finally went to a book store, I had forgot Benjamin Graham's name and bought another book with Buffett's printed recommendation on its front page. It was *Common Stocks and Uncommon Profits*, written by Phillip Fisher.

I Google-ed "Phillip Fisher" and it was then that I discovered that Buffett had two mentors and one of them was relatively less well-known. Fisher's book was a struggle for somebody new to investing (if only I had discovered Peter Lynch's *One Up on Wall Street* first!) but it gave me an excellent introduction to the finer points on investing in stocks. Since then, Philip Fisher's wise counsel has become part of my internal lodestone whenever I come across anything related to investing.

By 2010, my interest in investing had waned after National Service and University had entered my life. By a serendipitous stroke of luck while searching for investing-related articles on the internet, I came across The Motley Fool's website and was hooked. With The Motley Fool, I now had access to an entire online-community of thousands of like-minded and intelligent investors with which to share ideas and ask questions. Reading the articles and participating in the forums brought back the fire and with the help of Motley Fool's investment advisory subscription services, I finally made my first stock investments in October 2010 and have not looked back ever since. In the two years since, I have grown my investing knowledge by leaps and bounds with the help of The Motley Fool and friends I have made along the way.

It has been an exciting never-ending journey for me as I make progress each day to become an even better investor. I have benefitted immensely from the writings and self-less sharing from other professional investors and I hope I can pass the light on in my own little way by writing this book. So, here we (the authors) are, with *Invest Lah!*, a book that can improve your investing and take you onboard with us on the *SS Investing*!

~~~

Sudhan: My journey into the world of personal finance and investing started around October 2007 when I was in National Service (NS). I was 19 years old then. I was just promoted to be a Third Sergeant and wanted to learn how to budget my extra allowance prudently to prevent overspending. Thus, I made a trip to Popular bookstore to purchase some books on budgeting. As I strolled into Popular bookstore, to my left stood a section called "Popular Bestsellers". Perched on it was a book that caught my eyes instantly. The book was entitled *Rich Dad, Poor Dad* and it was by Robert Kiyosaki. The title was interesting so I picked it up to read the blurb on the back page and it seemed interesting. The blurb did not talk much about how the book could help me to budget my money but I bought the book anyway. I started reading the book only after it lay in my cupboard for a few weeks (I think the word "laziness" was coined specially for me). However, once I started reading, I was sucked into the book as the theories presented in the book were just mind-blowing. It was then that I decided I wanted to be financially free so that I could do whatever I want to do and not be hindered by money. After reading that book, I started reading more and more books on personal mastery, real estate and personal finance but I had not come into the world of stock investment yet. While my peers in National Service were playing games with their PSPs during their free time, I morphed into a bookworm.

Then in May 2008, I had the chance to go for a seminar called "National Achievers' Congress" at Singapore Expo organised by Success Resources. In the three-day seminar, I learnt a lot from T. Harv Eker, Joe Girard and Blair Singer and many other world-class speakers. I also had
~~~

a chance to go for a trading course the following month where I learnt various instruments such as forex, options, futures, stock trading, among others. I started trading forex and futures from then till end of 2008. I lost a substantial amount of money (it was substantial for me at that point of time as my NS allowance was only around $700). Trading made me go on an emotional rollercoaster and I decided it was not for me.

Just then, I came across a preview for a famous wealth mastery seminar at the end of 2008. I signed up for the course immediately after listening to the preview as it would teach me about personal finance, investing and many more, all in one course. I found the syllabus very comprehensive and decided it would be worth the money. The course started in March 2009 and it was a four-day course. It was there that I was introduced into the world of value investing and Warren Buffett. Before joining this course, my uncle had told me about stock investment and gave me a Peter Lynch book to read but I could not understand it at all. However, after the wealth mastery course, I became very intrigued by Warren Buffett's way of investment which was so simple to understand and was so logical. I have never looked back since. I started reading more books on value investing. I started looking at companies and used the methodology taught during the course.

Value investing made so much sense to me compared to trading and staring at charts and numbers. In June 2009, when I turned 21, I immediately went to open a brokerage account the following day of my birthday and I bought my first company a few weeks later. The company was Raffles Medical. I have to say I was really fortunate to have started investing in June 2009 as that was the time the market started to rally once again from the credit crunch of 2008/2009. I had the opportunity to start investing at rock-bottom prices. Ever since being introduced to value investing, I have not stopped reading more books and everyday is a learning journey for me. I have made a lot of mistakes in this journey but what is most important is that I have learnt a lot along the way. Mistakes make one a better investor. Yoggi Berra once said, "In theory there's no difference between theory and practice, but in practice there is". Experiencing the market is a thousand-fold better than just reading about the market in books and the internet.

In May 2010, I started my own personal finance and investing blog at http://financiallyfreenow.wordpress.com mainly to keep track of my journey in world of investing and personal finance. I am glad many have benefitted from reading my blog posts and encouraging comments keep me going. Sharing my knowledge selflessly is one of the ways I can give back to society.

I started on the journey to become financially free was I didn't want money to hinder what my family and I always wanted to pursue. Financial freedom brings freedom of choice. I want my wife and kids to have the best in their lives. I want to provide for my parents to the fullest as they have provided for me so much while I was young, even though they didn't have much for themselves. And, I find investing one of the best ways to achieve my goals.

I find investing very intriguing and it stimulates my mind. I feel like Sherlock Holmes when I research a company. Looking into a company's industry, track record, financial statements, hits and misses, etc. grips me a lot and I am glad that I have been introduced into the world of value investing. I hope you join me in this journey so that you and your loved ones will benefit from it.

~~~

Wei Lin: My parents had a subtle way of teaching me about budgeting since young. When I was in secondary school, they gave me pocket money on a monthly basis. As I moved into college, my allowance was given at the start of each year. This means that I have to plan out the entire year's budget in order not to run out of funds too early. Not an
~~~

easy task for a 16 year old, considering all the various distractions from bubble tea to gadgets to going out with friends.

By the time I entered the army, I had a pool of savings from my schooling days. According to the financial planning rule of thumb, I should only start investing when I have saved at least six months of my monthly expenses. So, I continued to save diligently while shopping around for financial products.

When I was 19, a catastrophic event in my family caused me to realize the importance of money, or more precisely, the importance of money management. I delved into the realm of financial planning, which led me to a shocking discovery. The financial planning industry in Singapore is generally commission based and this causes a conflict of interest. Dishonest agents might sometimes recommend a more expensive product so as to earn more commission or are forced to do so because of the company they represent. Well, after all, people don't buy insurance, they are sold.

Upon reaching my 21st birthday, I opened my first discretionary stock management account, where my fund manager will pick stocks on my behalf. At that point in time, I felt that I lacked expertise and experience, hence it would make more sense to appoint a professional money manager to invest on my behalf. I was dead wrong. Over the years, I've learnt that professional fund managers have far more limitations compared to retail investors, such as the type of stocks they can pick, investment time horizon, percentage allocation into individual stocks, just to name a few. My fund manager failed to outperform the market despite his "expertise" and "experience". Eventually, I closed my account and moved on to invest on my own.

Over the next couple of years, I continued to brush up on my investment knowledge by reading and learning from different people. My favourite book on value investing is *The Intelligent Investor* by Benjamin Graham. It opened up my mind to business and investing.

Besides reading extensively about value investing, business, behavioural finance and personal finance, I continued to attend seminars so as to meet like-minded friends.

So, here I am today writing this book together with my investing buddies, Ser Jing and Sudhan!

~~~
~~~

Introduction

Observe! Remember! Compare! – Alexander Graham Bell, on self-directed learning

Why the Title of the Book?

We came up with our title, *Invest Lah! — The Average Joe's Guide to Investing* because we want to show you, our reader, that investing is not something scary or overly complicated that requires an Ivy-League degree. None of us have a background in finance. Sudhan and Ser Jing both have Engineering backgrounds while Wei Lin is a Math graduate. We believe that everyone can master their own investing destiny so long as they approach it with the right mindset.

Why Write This Book?

We wrote this book because we felt that local readers can stand to benefit from a one-stop-shop for investing matters within a local context. Though our book is by no means a complete encyclopaedia (and no book can claim to be one), we believe it contains enough knowledge inside to help a complete novice stand on his own to make better-informed choices with regard to investing.

Ser Jing also feels behavioural finance has not been given enough attention among local investing books. It is important to know how our minds can play tricks on us and harm our investing results. In that spirit, we have decided to include a section on behavioural finance to give a brief glimpse of what it is all about, and why it is so important in investing.

Above all, we have benefitted greatly from the writings and interviews from investing masters and we hope to pass on the flame. Living expenses in Singapore are getting higher as we speak but yet, we keep seeing reports on how Singaporeans are not saving or investing enough to ensure a comfortable retirement. Furthermore, sad but preventable stories of stock-market excesses also pains us and we hope we can help to make our investing environment better by educating the public, one person at a time.

Ser Jing got a chance to look at a manual prepared by MAS for brokers who are taking mandatory exams for their particular line of work. He was appalled after noticing that *no* mention of successful investing philosophies as espoused by the likes of Warren Buffett, Benjamin Graham, Peter Lynch, etc. were mentioned in the manual. Brokers are probably the first point of contact to the stock market for many first-time investors but yet, even these brokers are not required to know an essential aspect of investing aside from technical analysis and other economy-related factors.

With this book, we hope that more people can appreciate what investing is about and hopefully, help enrich their lives by giving them the important head-start towards proper and prudent investing.

Now, let us bring you to where it all begins.... The mystifying and mysterious Stock Market.

The Stock Market

What Is It?

When you want to buy groceries, where do you go to? You go to the wet market. When you want to buy businesses, where do you go to? You go to the stock market. But wait, what is a stock, you might ask? A stock or share (these two terms can be used interchangeably) is essentially a small piece of a business. For example, if you own 10 shares in Company XYZ that is made up of 1,000 shares, you effectively own 1% of the company (10 shares dividend by 1,000). What this means is that you own 1% of every dollar of profit, every dollar of assets and every of dollar of debt that Company XYZ has. By owning stocks, you are in effect, a business owner! So, let us go back to the market where we can buy individual pieces of companies — the stock market. It is simply a collection of businesses for investors to buy and sell. Every country has its own unique stock market.

In Singapore, there are around 780 companies listed in the local stock market. There is only one exchange, Singapore Exchange (SGX), where companies can list. In comparison, bigger countries like the United States of America have more exchanges. In the US, there are three primary exchanges and they are the New York Stock Exchange (NYSE), the American Stock Exchange (AMEX) and the National Association of Securities Dealers Automated Quotation System (NASDAQ).

In SGX, there are various instruments listed and one of them is stocks. Other instruments include bonds, warrants, exchange-traded funds (ETF), real estate investment trusts (REITs) and business trusts. Under stocks itself, there are common stocks and preferred stocks. Whenever we mention "stocks" or "shares" in this book, we are referring to common stocks, unless otherwise specified.

If you want to know how the Singapore stock market is doing currently, what do you refer to? You refer to the Straits Times Index (The Straits Times Index is often abbreviated as the STI and more information about it can be found at http://www.ftse.com/Indices/FTSE_ST_Index_Series/). The STI tracks the performance of the top 30 companies in Singapore. Some of the companies in the STI include household names such as Singapore Airlines (SIA), DBS Bank Limited (DBS), Singapore Telecommunications Limited (Singtel), Singapore Press Holdings (SPH), Starhub and SGX itself. The companies in the STI are also sometimes referred to as "blue-chip" companies. They are likened to the huge bodybuilders in a gym whereas the smaller companies are the scrawny guys with lots of potential to grow bigger.

Why Companies List and How Do We Benefit?

Suppose a local private company called XYZ Corporation is doing so well that it wants to expand its business beyond its shores. It wants to expand to China, the US, and Australia. However, it does not have much capital to expand. What can it do? It can borrow money. One way is to borrow money from the bank and the other is to borrow money from investors.

The banks might not want to lend huge sums of money to XYZ Corporation as they are not established enough and the banks might deem the company "risky". The alternative is to borrow money from investors like us. Investors can come from a private pool or public pool.

Private investors can own part of the company without the company being listed. However, if XYZ Corporation wants to access money from public investors like us, it has to list itself in an exchange like SGX and become a public company. Now let us digress a little on the difference between private and public investing. The main difference between a private and public company is how the latter's shares are quoted on a stock exchange. Meaning, the public company's shares are given a market value every day on the stock exchange as investors from all corners of the globe buy and sell its shares in *full view of the public*. Private companies, on the other hand, do not have its shares quoted daily in the stock exchanges. Private businesses can range from the humble chicken rice stall in your favourite hawker centre to mega conglomerates like the diamond-sellers De Beers. You can invest in them, but the process is *a lot* more laborious than investing in publicly traded companies.

That's because shares in private companies are usually only available for purchase in special arrangements set up by banks for their clients (other corporations or wealthy individuals). For example, only very wealthy individuals or Venture Capital firms (VCs are basically a collection of money from different investors that are managed by a 'fund manager'. These VC firms then find promising start-ups to invest in.) were able to invest in Facebook's stock before it became a publicly traded company on the NASDAQ stock exchange in the USA on May 2012.

Despite the difficulty in investing in private companies, and the lack of daily quotations on private companies' shares, there is one *very important fact* that should be remembered. That is, evaluating the value of a private company involves the study of its financials, its management teams and its business model. That is *no different* from how public businesses should be analysed even though its stock gets quoted daily on an exchange. This should be a not-so-subtle hint that stock exchanges might get the true value (or intrinsic value) of a public company wrong. And as investors in publicly listed companies, the time to act is precisely when there is a severe disconnect between a market quotation and the intrinsic value of a public company's stock.

Now, back to XYZ Corporation. When it wants to list itself on a stock exchange, it has to go through an Initial Public Offering (IPO) process where the shares of the company are sold to the public. You might have heard of the term IPO in the press previously. The biggest talked-about IPO in the past year, which did not materialize, was that of Manchester United.

Now, back to XYZ Corporation, why would investors want to buy shares in XYZ Corporation? The main reason to buy shares of XYZ Corporation is to profit from it. No one buys a company's shares proclaiming, "I want to buy the shares so that I can lose money in the future. Woohoo!" (if they do, please ask them to read this book!). When you buy shares, you become a partial owner of the company. Your stake in the company depends on the number of shares you hold as a percentage of the total number of shares the firm has issued.

Profiting from investing in shares can come in two forms. One is through capital appreciation, where you buy low and sell high. Capital appreciation occurs as the company grows and its cash profits increase. The company becomes more attractive to investors. The other is through passive income in the form of dividends, where cash is returned to shareholders from the profits the company makes. Do note that not all companies pay dividends.

To illustrate what is capital appreciation and dividends, let's say you bought 1 lot[1] of a locally listed company called Vicom during

---

[1] To invest in the local market, one has to buy 1,000 shares of a company (some companies trade in other quantities) which is also known as one board lot. Unlike in the US where one called buy just one share of a company, investors investing in the Singapore market cannot do so.

the market crash in 2009 at $1,500 and you sold it off in 2012 at $4,000. You made a profit of $2,500 when you only invested $1,500. The total capital appreciation you got was 167% [($2,500/$1,500) × 100%]. In the meantime, Vicom also paid dividends to the tune of around $450 for every lot of shares owned. The total returns, inclusive of capital appreciation and dividends, is at $2,950 ($2,500 + $450) or 197% [($2,950/$1,500) × 100%].

As a part-owner of a company, you are entitled to attend the Annual General Meeting (AGM) and vote on corporate matters. The AGM is held after every financial year of the company.

How Do Stocks Trade?

Once XYZ Corporation becomes listed, it starts trading in SGX. Trading means the stock can be bought and sold at any time and the trading hours are from 9am to 5pm[2]. Let's say the company's IPO price was at $1 and it started to trade at the same price on the first day of being listed. A point movement for XYZ Corporation would be movement by 0.5 cent[2]. During trading hours, the stock price can move up, move down or stay stagnant. Price moves up and down due to the enthusiasm of buyers and the desperation of sellers respectively or put in economic terms, prices move because of the supply and demand of the shares.

Important Questions to ponder about...

1. How do people profit from the stock market?
2. Why do companies IPO?
3. What do you think is the long term relationship between the returns of a particular stock and the underlying business?

---

[2] More about the trading hours, price movements, corporate actions and many more will be covered in the later part of the book.

Why Bother to Invest?

> *Compound interest is the eighth wonder of the world. He who understands it, earns it ... he who doesn't ... pays it* — Albert Einstein

Stay Ahead of Taxes and Inflation

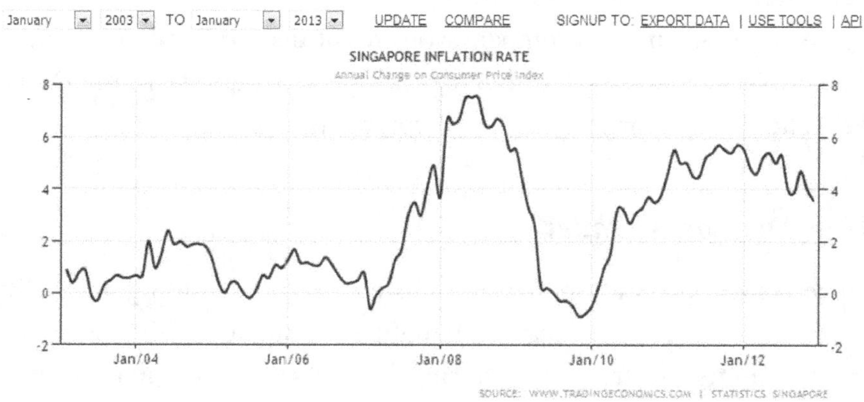

Figure 1.1 Singapore Inflation Rate

Source: Adapted from http://www.tradingeconomics.com/singapore/inflation-cpi.

The above chart shows the inflation rate in Singapore for the past ten years. In Singapore, the inflation rate measures a broad increase or decrease in prices that consumers pay for a standard basket of goods.

As of November 2012, the inflation rate in Singapore, reported by the Department of Statistics Singapore, was at 3.60%. Historically, from 1962 until 2012, Singapore's Inflation Rate averaged 2.82% reaching a record high of 34% in March of 1974 and a record low of −3.10% in September of 1976.

So how does inflation affect us? Well, in the long run, goods and services become more expensive and if our money does not grow at a rate higher than that of inflation, our purchasing power decreases. This is why we always hear our parents complaining that the cost of a plate of chicken rice has tripled or even quadrupled over the years! As such, it would be prudent for investors to grow their money at a rate higher than that of inflation so as to retain purchasing power over time.

Power of Compounding

Albert Einstein called compound interest the "greatest mathematical discovery of all time". So what inspired him to say that? Let's consider the table below, which depicts the returns from the common financial instruments that people commonly use. Have a look at the ending amount of money after investing $1,000 per annum for 30 years.

After compounding for five years, the difference between the various instruments is minimal. However, after compounding for 30 years, the difference is staggering.

Why is the difference between a few percentage points of return so substantial after long periods of time? This is the miraculous power of compounding. When your investments start to generate positive returns and those returns start to generate even more money, your investment can grow very quickly. Increase the time period or the rate of return, and your results will escalate exponentially.

As a long-term investor, time is your greatest ally. Start investing as early as possible to take full advantage of the power of compounding. And we feel the stock market is one of the best places to invest money, along with the property market (but we shall not go into a debate between the relative merits of property investing versus stock market investing). We have already given a basic primer on what the stock market is all about. Remember — it is a place where we can buy partial ownership of businesses and not just to speculate on the prices of stock tickers.

Now, let's turn our sights to some common myths you might have heard about the stock market and why they are what they're called — *Myths*.

Table 1.1 Table of Returns

Annualized Returns	Instrument	1 yr	5 yr	10 yr	15 yr	20 yr	25 yr	30 yr
0.1%	Local Bank Savings Rate	1,000	5010.01	10045.12	15105.46	20191.14	25302.31	30439.09
0.25%	Fixed Deposit	1,000	5025.06	10113.25	15265.37	20482.20	25764.57	31113.31
8%	STI Return	1,000	5866.60	14486.56	27152.11	45761.96	73105.94	113283.21

Wei Lin thinks that we should invest to retain our purchasing power over time. Inflation is like a plague that slowly eats away the value of our money. The power of compounding can work either in our favour, when we invest in fantastic businesses, or against us when we get ourselves in debt.

Important Questions to ponder about…

1. What does investing mean to you?
2. What is the difference between investing and speculating?
3. Does a stock that fluctuates greatly in price constitute more risk as compared to one that does not fluctuate much?

Myths of Investing

"Wall Street is the only place that people ride to in a Rolls Royce to get advice from those who take the subway." — Warren Buffett

"In Professionals We Trust"

In a society where education and academic qualifications are highly regarded, it is understandable for people to look for the brightest and most qualified professionals to manage their money.

However, based on an article published by CNN Money on 23 February 2012, 79% of fund managers did not beat the Standard & Poor's

Index in year 2011 (http://money.cnn.com/2012/02/23/pf/fund_manager_performance.moneymag/index.htm). In fact, as a whole, it was their worst performance since 1997. The Standard & Poor's Index is taken as a proxy for the performance of the entire stock market in the USA and a comparison of a fund manager's (or unit trust manager) performance against the stock market's performance is important. Why? Because if you invest in those funds, the fund managers will charge you management fees, which are usually in place regardless of whether you make money or not. If the fund managers are not able to outperform the market, you are being treated very unfairly because there is an extremely easy access to investment instruments that can track the stock market's overall movement very well: index funds and unit trusts. Before we digress, let's move back to why we think "In Professionals We Trust" is purely a myth.

If we may propose, here are some of the reasons why professionals fail to beat the market. There are plenty of restrictions in the fund management industry that retail investors might be unaware of. For example, fund managers might be restricted on the percentage of a fund which they can allocate to a single stock.

Also, fund managers might be only allowed to pick certain companies for their portfolios. They can be restricted based on the market capitalization of the company, for example. This narrows down the stock universe in which he is allowed to work with. This might not make sense, depending on his area of expertise.

Furthermore, they are required to be close to fully invested *at all times*. Now, imagine a situation where a fund manager feels that stocks are *not* attractive at all but there's nothing he can do about it.

The emphasis on diversification and correlation between individual stock holdings makes decision-making for fund managers all the more difficult. Can you imagine picking a business just because it moves exactly the opposite to say the price of gold? How ridiculous does that sound? These are the hand-cuffs that fund managers have to deal with in their industry and you, as an investor, are forced to pick up the slack.

"If You Want to Earn Higher Returns, You Have to Take More Risk"

Well, this really depends on the individual's definition of risk. Conventionally, academics define financial risk using beta. Beta is defined as the correlation of an asset's volatility with respect to the benchmark that it is being compared to, which usually refers to a stock market index. In simple terms, academics prefer to measure risk in terms of relative volatility. And in simpler terms, volatility simply means "how much will share prices move for a given period of time".

However, this measure of risk does not make any sense for investors who wish to purchase a bigger slice of a great business at a cheaper price. If so, then how is the increased movement of prices a bad thing?

Wei Lin (and Ser Jing and Sudhan, for the matter) thinks that in the long run, investors should only be concerned with one type of risk, that is, the risk of total permanent loss of capital. This risk can be reduced via various methods of security analysis, such as balance sheet analysis (refer to Section 2: The Numbers).

To quote Howard Marks of Oaktree Capital, *You can invest in the best companies in America and have a bad experience, or you can invest in the worst companies in America and have a good experience. So the lesson is clear: it's not asset quality that determines investment risk. The bottom line on this is simple. No asset is so good that it can't be bid up to the point where it's overpriced and thus dangerous. And few assets are so bad that they can't become underpriced and thus safe. Since participants set security prices, it's their behaviour that creates most of the risk in investing.*

To be fair, it is not easy to watch stock prices swing up and down violently, sometimes for perfectly legitimate reasons, other times for no real reason. But, once we understand the idea that risk involves losing capital on a *permanent* basis, it can make investing that much less stressful because as investors, we are concerned with what is going on with a business — and we will go through the anatomy of being an investor in due course.

Wei Lin feels that if we re-think our conventional definition of risk, which is the measure of volatility of the stock price with respect to the market, then perhaps we can invest more prudently and in the process, we can achieve better returns with lower risk.

"Diversification is ALWAYS Good"

Consider this, suppose you're the Principal of a primary school and you're tasked to pick out students which you think will outperform the rest in terms of academic results over the next 10 years.

Will you:

(A) Do in-depth research by speaking to various people (e.g. peers, teachers, and parents), look at the student's past year performance and select say 10–15 students which you think have a relatively high chance of success? Or,
(B) Select a large number of students and take the average?

The truth is that if you know your students well enough, diversification just doesn't make sense. Wei Lin believes the same applies to investing. If you're able to understand the businesses that you own and take the effort to understand and evaluate them from time to time, then perhaps you want to think about how to concentrate your holdings rather than diversify them.

Wei Lin thinks that you should diversify only to the extent that it provides you with a good night's rest and not use it as a lazy excuse to hedge against ignorance. For an investor who does his due diligence, 10–15 stocks should provide adequate diversification.

Studies done by James Montier from the investing firm GMO have also shown that a portfolio of 30–40 stocks will have almost the same volatility as the broad stock market itself. Volatility, as we mentioned earlier, is not really "risk", but it can and does affect people's emotions with regard to investing and if a 30–40 stock portfolio can achieve the same kind of volatility as the stock market, it can help lessen any harmful emotional consequences that come with a more concentrated portfolio.

The bottom-line conclusion is this: Diversification only makes sense up to a point.

"The More Updated You Are About Market News, the Better Your Chances for Higher Returns"

We're not too sure about you, but we've always been a major skeptic of weather reports. Have you ever met a weatherman that has consistently predicted the weather over the course of his career? The world is a dynamic ecosystem of multivariables which are in constant interaction with one another. It is difficult, if not impossible, to come up with any reasonable prediction for the direction of the stock market or any particular stock in the short run. That would be the equivalent of peering through a crystal ball, which I suspect only Professor Dumbledore has one.

As such, investors should be undiscerned about short-term macroeconomic trends and continue to focus on the long-term value of the businesses they own. Consider this quote from Warren Buffett's 1994 Berkshire Hathaway Shareholder Letter.

We try to price, rather than time, purchases. In our view, it is folly to forego buying shares in an outstanding business whose long-term future is predictable, because of short-term worries about an economy or a stock market that we know to be unpredictable. Why scrap an informed decision because of an uninformed guess?

"The More Actively You Manage Your Portfolio, the Higher Your Returns"

Expenses are the foe of an investor. The more frequently you hop in and out of businesses, the more expenses you will incur in terms of brokerage commissions as well as capital gains tax (for US companies).

Hence, you should be looking to use a low-cost broker. Placing your orders online, as compared to over the phone, also usually leads to lower commissions. We will be covering more on buying and selling shares in Singapore in Section 5.

Also, buy-and-hold investors are able to capture the full dividends which come along with the stock they own. Conversely, investors who actively switch from one popular stock to the other end up missing out on the dividend payments.

Let's also consider a stock-market index tracker. An index tracker aims to mimic the movement of a stock market index. A stock market index is essentially a group of stocks that market folks group together to represent something. For example, if we wanted to see how the overall stock market in Singapore fared, we could use the FTSE Straits Times Index or the FTSE All-Share Index as a close proxy for how the overall stock market in Singapore fared.

So, if an investor had invested in the SPDR Straits Times Index Exchange Traded Fund on Dec 2002 and held on till Dec 2012, he would have gotten cumulative returns of 136% simply by buying and holding, without making any transactions. To double your money after 10 years without lifting a finger sounds like a pretty good deal to us!

Now that we have debunked some myths in investing, let us get on to the real deal — what does it mean to be an investor?

Wei Lin thinks that we are exposed to a myriad of financial news everyday and it is important that we learn to discern between fact and opinion. Never take any words for granted just because someone claims to be an expert on that matter. Always do your homework before investing.

Important Questions to ponder about…

1. Does your financial advisor recommend you to purchase a diversified portfolio of funds?
2. How does he/she evaluate which fund is suitable for purchase and how has his/her own portfolio performed over the years? Has it been outperforming the index?
3. What are some common financial views offered by the ten people you mix around with most often? Can you discern between the facts and opinions?

Prudent Investing

The most important thing we ever learn at school is the fact that the most important things can't be learned at school

— Haruki Murakami

Let's play a game (yes, I know it sounds like Jigsaw!). The following is a short questionnaire and we want you to answer them truthfully.

1. Do you buy stocks based on what your friends, relatives or stock analysts say?
2. Do you invest in penny stocks because they are cheap, meaning you do not have to come up with lots of money to buy them?
3. Do you view stocks selling at more than \$1 as expensive and those selling below \$1 as cheap?
4. Do you buy stocks without researching into what the company does as it does not matter?
5. Do you buy stocks just because the particular company has been giving good dividends for the past five years?

If most of the answers above were a resounding "Yes!" then this section of the book is just for you. You are ready to learn more about Prudent Investing and help you Invest Lah!

Before we hit the road running, it is paramount we have a small shift in our mindset to that of a prudent investor. All this while, you might have viewed stocks as pieces of paper with prices going up and down almost daily. If we shout out "Starhub!", for example, if the first thing that comes up in your mind is the latest stock price and subsequently the stock prices of the past few days of Starhub, you most probably view stocks as pieces of paper to be traded. That is the main mindset we have to change for us to prosper in Prudent Investing. Prudent investors view stocks as businesses. Businesses take time to grow and prosper and the value of the business does not fluctuate daily, like the stock price. Once we have got this mindset in place, we are ready to rock and roll...

What Is Prudent Investing?

When we started out on our journey as investors, we read widely. We read books and articles written by famous financial academics, professional investors as well as financial writers. There was a whole gamut of investing philosophies that have been put on paper, such as *Value Investing, Growth Investing, Growth at Reasonable Prices, Contrarian Investing,* etc. These investing philosophies were all successfully applied to the stock market by their various practitioners, who are all highly revered among the investing community. Famous names attached to *Value Investing* include Benjamin Graham, Walter Schloss, Seth Klarman and of course, Warren Buffett. *Growth Investing* has its apostle in Phillip Fisher, while Peter Lynch was a widely acknowledged investing legend that practised *Growth at Reasonable Prices.* Lesser known but still extremely successful *Contrarian Investing* proponents include John Neff and David Dreman.

As we came to know the methods, mind-sets and philosophy of these investors, we realised that at the forefront of all successful investing philosophies lay a common underlying theme — *Investors look at stocks as a piece of a business*! As Peter Lynch, said, *Behind every stock is a company. Find out what it is doing.* It is an extremely powerful concept to have when you realise that there is actually a slow-changing anchor (the business) attached to a fast-moving object (the stock price of a company) that can allow you to make good investing decisions.

With the powerful anchoring thought that investing is looking at stocks as a piece of business, we started to weave together aspects of the different philosophies that resonate with our own *temperament, psyche* and *unique skill sets* and this allows us to pass the *sleep-at-night* test. The *sleep-at-night* test is a very important lesson that Ser Jing learnt from The Motley Fool community and it basically means that if the investing process is sound and fits the individual's *temperament, psyche* and *unique skill sets*, the investor can sleep soundly at night without worrying about short-term price-fluctuations of his investments in the public markets.

The name *Prudent Investing* thus came about not because we wanted to reinvent the wheel (we do not want to and also do not see ourselves as being qualified enough to do so) but because we thought (1) investing should be done with careful consideration of the underlying *fundamentals* of the business (the common theme among all the different investment philosophies), (2) pass the *sleep-at-night* test if investing was done prudently and (3) that it is important for each of you to work with the investing philosophy that suits you best and not be pigeon-holed into thinking that there is only one fundamentals-based strategy to go about investing. With this said, we would now like to bring to you what we, as prudent investors, like to consider when we go about investing in stocks. Prudent Investing involves studying the business, management and potential future catalysts (The Story), analysing the financial statements and determining the value of the business (The Numbers) and keeping our mind in check to prevent our portfolio from getting jeopardized (The Mind).

Prudent Investing is one whole package and the parts cannot stand alone. The main aspect of Prudent Investing is to buy businesses that are selling below its intrinsic value, a concept which will be explored further in The Numbers. Prudent Investing also involves fundamental analysis of a business as opposed to technical analysis where absolute price and volume are used to buy stocks. We only cover fundamental analysis in this book. Fundamental analysis, as the name suggests, involves looking at the fundamentals of a business. The Story part forms the qualitative aspect of fundamental analysis and The Numbers part forms the quantitative aspect of fundamental analysis.

Following is a table of comparison between Prudent Investors and traders:

	Prudent Investors	**Traders**
Tools of the Trade	Fundamental analysis	Technical analysis
Stock Market Fluctuations	Not bothered about daily price fluctuations	Rely on price fluctuations without regard for value of the business
Time Horizon	Long-term (five years or more)	Short-term (can even be in minutes)
Portfolio Turnover Rate	Low	High

Risk

Many deem investing as risky. During the 2008/2009 financial crisis, some retirees in Singapore lost their entire life savings investing in Lehman Minibonds. Going further back, during the Asian Financial Crisis back in 1997, many had lost a substantial amount of money in the stock market. Due to these episodes, many have the notion that investing must be left to the professionals and that it is not suitable for laymen like us. What we believe is that investing is not risky if we know what we are investing in. If we really take the time to understand the business and know the value of the business, we can actually have the courage and conviction to buy more when prices come down. Warren Buffett said that risk comes from not knowing what one is doing. If you understand what you are doing, you take the risk out of the equation, don't you? Finance students in the university learn that risk is measured in terms of beta. Beta, as we mentioned earlier, is a measure of the volatility of a security in comparison to the market as a whole. High volatility equates to high beta or high risk (in financial academic terms) but we beg to differ. Our view is that volatility is your friend and not your foe to be afraid of. With high volatility, stocks have the chance to drop more and this presents an opportunity for prudent investors to buy more of a wonderful business. Take, for example, that ABC Company has an intrinsic value of $25 but is trading at $20. This may be an attractive investment. If the stock drops to $10, which makes the stock more volatile, and hence more "risky", the stock actually becomes a more attractive investment. The declining price becomes an even better bargain!

Benjamin Graham once quipped about price volatility — "Price fluctuations have only one significant meaning for the true investor. They provide him with an opportunity to buy wisely when prices fall sharply and to sell wisely when they advance a great deal. At other times he will do better if he forgets about the stock market and pays attention to...the operating results of his companies."

While Graham's student, Warren Buffett, had this to ask to get us thinking, in his 1997 Berkshire Hathaway's Shareholder Letter: *If you plan to eat hamburgers throughout your life and are not a cattle producer, should you wish for higher or lower prices for beef? Likewise, if you are going to buy a car from time to time but are not an auto manufacturer, should you prefer higher or lower car prices? These questions, of course, answer themselves. But now for the final exam: If you expect to be a net saver during the next five years, should you hope for a higher or lower stock market during that period?* Many investors get this one wrong. Even though they are going to be net buyers of stocks for many years to come, they are elated when stock prices rise and depressed when they fall. In effect, they rejoice because prices have risen for the "hamburgers" they will soon be buying. This reaction makes no sense. Only those who will be sellers of equities in the near future should be happy at seeing stocks rise. Prospective purchasers should much prefer sinking prices."

If you think about it, everything has risks. Even crossing the road has risks. However, the risks can be minimized by looking left, right and right again before crossing. The same analogy can be used in investing. In investing, we increase the probability of winning and decrease the chances of going wrong but knowing what we are doing (researching thoroughly in the business before putting our hard-earned money in).

If your investment strategy relies on buying stocks with no regard for the underlying company's value, you are taking on huge risks. If you buy shares only when they are rising to their 52-week high price and sell in panic every time the prices fall, you run the risk of buying high, selling low — a sure way to lose money in the long-term. By knowing what you are doing and doing it prudently, you minimize the risks and maximize the returns. This is a sure way to make money in the long-term.

Business Behind the Ticker Symbol

Benjamin Graham once mentioned that *investment is most intelligent when it is most businesslike. Stock market investment is not merely buying pieces of paper with the prices fluctuating daily. Behind the stock price and the ticker symbol, there is a business. Like mentioned right at the start, businesses take time to flourish and fundamentals do not change overnight, unlike a stock price.*

When you flip open the "Money" section of the Straits Times, you can find the previous day's prices of some of the blue-chip companies. Let's say SIA Engineering closed at $3.45 yesterday. The 52-week high price was $4.38 and the 52-week low price was $3.34. How come there are such huge changes in the price within one year? Can the value of the SIA Engineering business change so much within one year?

Certainly not. The stock price moves according to the buyers and sellers in the market (supply and demand) but the value of the business does not change every second, like the stock price. Stock price is not (a big, fat, gigantic, humongous capital NOT) equal to the value of the business. Paying too high a price for too little a value will set you on a disappointing trip. In the short term, the stock market behaves like a voting machine, but in the long term, it acts like a weighing machine. This means that *the price of the stock is never equal to the value of the business in the short-term. In the long-term, the price and the value will converge.*

Following is a table of summary of what we have mentioned above:

	Stocks	**Businesses**
Unit of Measurement	Price	Value
Accuracy of Measurement	Precise (and often wrong)	Approximate (but usually right)
Rate of Change	Every few seconds or milliseconds even	A few times a year (or lesser)
Reason for Change	Different price offered by someone who doesn't own it (supply and demand)	Different amount of cash is produced for the people who own it

Mr. Market and His Tantrums

We stated above that the main aspect of Prudent Investing is to buy businesses that are selling below its intrinsic value. That is to say, we want to buy businesses that are selling for 50 cents when the actual worth is a dollar. How is this possible? Before we tackle that predicament, we have to introduce you to the concept of "Mr. Market".

The term Mr. Market was coined by Benjamin Graham in 1949 in his famous book called *The Intelligent Investor*. The following quote sums up his philosophy:

> *Imagine you had a partner in a private business named Mr. Market. Mr. Market, the obliging fellow that he is, shows up daily to tell you what he thinks your interest in the business is worth. On most days, the price he quotes is reasonable and justified by the business's prospects. However, Mr. Market suffers from some rather incurable emotional problems; you see, he is very temperamental. When Mr. Market is overcome by boundless optimism or bottomless pessimism, he will quote you a price that seems to you a little short of silly. As an intelligent investor, you should not fall under Mr. Market's influence, but rather you should learn to take advantage of him. The value of your interest should be determined by rationally appraising the business's prospects, and you can happily sell when Mr. Market quotes you a ridiculously high price and buy when he quotes you an absurdly low price. The best part of your association with Mr. Market is that he does not care how many times you take advantage of him. No matter how many times you saddle him with losses or rob him of gains, he will arrive the next day ready to do business with you again.*

There you go. You do not have to buy a stock at a ridiculously high price. The stock market exists to serve us and not to guide our decisions. Prudent Investing involves patience — lots of it. We have to be patient to wait for the stock price to come below our *estimate* of intrinsic value (more on that in The Numbers). Back to your question on how it is possible for the stock price to come below the value of the business. This phenomenon happens quite a couple of times — all due to the tantrums of Mr. Market. It can happen during a market crash, during a slight correction of the market or during a temporary one-time solvable problem.

A stock market crash usually means that the index drops more than 10% in a few days. Statistically, this happens once around every five years as seen from The National Bureau of Economic Research website. If there is a stock market crash, a recession usually follows as the market is usually a leading indicator of the economy. During such a time, a great opportunity is presented to grab businesses at bargain prices. It is like the "Great Singapore Sale" for stocks! During the recent 2008–2009 economic crisis, Straits Times reported that the number of millionaires in Singapore increased by 32.7%. Wonderful businesses like Vicom, Raffles Medical Group and Boustead were selling way below their intrinsic values. If you had bought shares in those companies then, you could have made a considerable sum of money! Do not worry though. Mark Twain once said that "*History* doesn't repeat itself, but it does rhyme." The economy works in cycles and opportunities will surely be presented in the future.

A correction usually means that the index drops less than 10% over a few days. It is less pronounced than a market crash. Corrections also give opportunities for us to buy stocks on the cheap but to a lesser extent usually.

When an outstanding business is affected by a temporary one-time solvable problem, it can be a huge opportunity to invest in the company. *A great investment opportunity occurs when a marvellous business encounters a one-time huge, but solvable, problem.* — Warren Buffett. Examples are abound of such instances. One such famous case in Singapore is Osim. Its share price plunged to a low of $0.05 in early 2009 due to losses in an investment based in USA, Brookstone. The recession in 2008–2009 hugely affected the business in USA and this caused a massive hit in the share price. However, Osim had learnt from the investment and has written off the business. If there had not been any losses in Brookstone, Osim would have had a profitable year in financial year 2008 (results were announced around February 2009). The share price has since recovered and the currently it stands at $1.72 (at the time of writing). Another example is Boustead. Boustead's share price was hit in 2011 due to the foray into Libya. On hindsight, it was not a good decision due to the infamous black-swan event — civil war. The share price dropped to a low of around $0.80 then. Currently, the share price is at $1.015.

Even one of Warren Bufffet's greatest investments came amid a one-time solvable problem. In 1963, a "salad oil" scandal occurred when American Express found that $60 million lent against collateral were mostly sea water instead of salad oil. The borrower was bankrupt and American Express had to take a loss of $60 million.

Buffett analysed the situation and found that the trust in American Express travellers' check and charge cards were unaffected. The company's intrinsic value was also higher than the share price then. He saw virtually no downside and maximum upside. He invested 40% of the net worth of the Buffett Partnership, or roughly $13 million. Buffett bought 5% of American Express stock, which had collapsed to $35 a share from a high of more than $62. In the following two years, the stock price of American Express tripled and the Buffett Partnership reportedly sold out with a $20 million profit.

The morale of the story is to be a contrarian and be greedy when others are fearful! Investing during a market crash, during a slight correction of the market or during a temporary one-time solvable problem provides the highest potential for upside.

Prudent Investing Works

Investors following Prudent Investing get decent returns as the market starts to recognize the value in the business. Prudent Investors buy companies when Mr. Market throws a tantrum and when Mr. Market realises his mistake, he tends to re-rate the company higher, sending the stock price much higher. Being a contrarian pays!

The share price of a company rises due to higher expectations of the company in the future. Prudent Investors look for future growth drivers that will allow a re-rating of the stock. Future growth drivers of a company can include expanding the business into another country, coming up with new product mixes, innovating the current product line, etc.

The next few examples show companies that have had a rise in stock price after its stock price had languished for a long while.

The first example is that of Kingsmen Creatives. Kingsmen Creatives is an interior and exhibition design company. Kingsmen's share price has been hovering for the longest time at the 55–62 cents range from

November 2009 to January 2012. Its share price went higher than this range in mid-February 2012 when a Dutch fund company "showed hand" and announced they hold 5% of Kingsmen Creatives. Since then, the share price has never looked back and it has gotten challenging for savvy investors to accumulate shares in Kingsmen. The share price of Kingsmen is 79.5 cents (at the time of writing).

The next two examples are that of listed companies that have become privatized. First up is Thomson Medical Centre (TMC). TMC is a private hospital with comprehensive range of services with focus in Obstetrics and Gynaecology and paediatric services. On 29th October 2010, Peter Lim, a renowned local investor, decided to privatize the listed company at $1.75 per share. The share price was at a 62% premium over the last traded price. Second is Cerebos. Readers will be familiar with this company as they produce the famous Brands Chicken Essence. Cerebos has been privatized at $6.60 per share and this was 22.7% higher than the last traded price.

An article by Warren Buffet, "The Superinvestors of Graham–and-Doddsville", makes an excellent read for those who want to know why such an investment works and why it is not pure luck!

Analysing the Management the Easy Way

When we invest in stocks, we are putting our hard-earned money into the hands of management of the business. Would you want to invest in a company if the company is run by unscrupulous individuals? Of course not! Therefore, we need to scrutinize the management for their integrity and competence. Warren Buffett once quipped that "In evaluating people, you look for three qualities: integrity, intelligence, and energy. And if you don't have the first, the other two will kill you". A dishonest management will be more concerned about dressing up the financial statements for short-term gains rather than building the business for long-term prosperity.

There are various ways to find out about the management of a business. The easiest way by far is to Google the name of the Chief Executive Officer (CEO) and adding words like "honest", "integrity", "ethical", "dishonest", "fraud", etc. From the Google searches, we would be able to find websites and articles showing the integrity, or lack thereof, of the management.

Another way is to look at the annual report of the business and look at the percentage of ownership of the company by the management. If the management owns a huge part of the business, we can be assured that the management's decisions will be aligned with that of the shareholders. Since most of the CEO's wealth is tied up to the business, he will not do anything detrimental to the business which will affect minor shareholders, like us.

Insider buying can also send a huge signal about the potential of the business. Insiders are a company's officers, directors, relatives, substantial shareholders or anyone else with access to key company information before it's made available to the public. When an insider is buying into a company, it can mean only one thing — that the person's belief in the company has strengthened and that it will deliver more value in the future. On the other hand, insider selling can mean many things. When an insider sells a company, it can mean that he is taking some profit off the table, he needs the money for personal reasons or he knows something that the rest do not know. When one insider sells, it usually does not raise a red flag. However, when there is a mass exodus of insiders from the company, it most probably means something really bad is brewing in the company! When the percentage of ownership of a substantial shareholder changes by 1% (rounded down), it is mandatory that he files a report with SGX within two business days. Prudent Investors can then go to the SGX website to obtain the necessary information.

The annual report will also contain a section on remuneration of the management. Check the compensation package of the management and directors to ensure they are not overly paid. This can be done by cross-checking the compensation with that of the competitors of the company.

Analysing the Management the "Harder" Way — Attending the Annual General Meeting

Annual General Meetings (AGMs) are conducted after every financial year where the directors and management of a company will report the company's performance to their shareholders. It happens usually one to two months after the release of results of the full financial year. If you are not a shareholder of a company but are interested to attend the AGM, you can email the Investor Relations department and request to attend the AGM as an observer. However, for most companies, you will not be allowed to ask questions as an observer.

Attending AGMs is highly recommended as one can observe subtle clues about management that may not be possible to know just by reading annual reports. It also allows the investor to meet the management face-to-face and ask them questions. Before attending an AGM, Prudent Investors should read through the latest annual report and the financial statements so that the time spent at the AGM will be worthwhile.

Once at an AGM, instead of eying the sumptuous buffet spread, grab a good seat just in front of the management so that you can observe the body language of the management when someone hits the nail by posing difficult questions about the business.

Once the AGM has started, notice how the meeting generally is conducted. Is it conducted in a business-like way with decorum? There will be time given to ask questions. Some of the questions you can ask are:

- What are some of the mistakes you have done over the past year and how did you rectify them?
- Why do customers buy your products over those of your competitors?

- What are you doing that your competitors aren't doing yet?
- What is the current biggest threat to the company and industry?
- What are the future growth plans in place to increase shareholders' value?
- From the time an initial customer prospect is identified, how long does it take to close the sale?
- Are there any important sectors of your market which you don't address?
- Are there any new entrants into the market in the last two years?
- Is there any seasonality in your business other than as reflected in orders and backlog?
- Is the marketing conducted any differently overseas?
- What is the long-term outlook of the company? Where do you see yourself 5 to 10 years into the future?
- What are your long-term objectives for profit margins and how do you intend to achieve those goals?
- Over the next few years, how would you expect the components of your income statement to change in relation to each other?
- Should one expect to see major acquisitions or divestitures as part of your plan for the short-term?
- Do you envision any major functional additions to the senior management staff?
- What are you plans for capital expenditures for the next few years and what specific product areas do you plan to stress?
- What are you currently spending your money on in R&D?

You can also ask other company-specific questions that bother you. For example, if the company took on excessive debt for the year without any future growth plans in place, you can ask the company the rationale for doing so.

After the AGM, the management will usually be lingering around the buffet spread area to interact with shareholders. You can ask more questions then. Notice how the managers and directors carry themselves when interacting with people. Are they humble? Are they approachable and friendly? Are they forthcoming?

Furthermore, you can also do scuttlebutt (don't worry, more on scuttlebutt soon!) and pose questions to the non-shareholders and non-stakeholders like cleaners, deliverymen, etc. on how the management interacts with them. Do they treat them with respect and smile at them? Are they friendly towards them? This can be one of the best ways to uncover the integrity of the management.

We've given you a glimpse of what it's like to analyse the leaders of a business, now, let us analyse the business itself, starting with a mighty castle in the middle of a tranquil lake.

Important Questions to ponder about...

1. What do you think are the main differences between a trader and an investor? Do you see yourself as a trader or as an investor?
2. Does the volatility of your portfolio cause you to lose sleep at night?
3. What does prudent investing mean to you?

Economic Moats

In business, I look for economic castles protected by unbreachable moats.
— Warren Buffett

The concept of an Economic Moat might not have originated from Warren Buffett, but he and his business partner, Charlie Munger, certainly popularised the phrase among the investment community. It was said that buying cigar-butt companies — very cheap, totally unloved stocks that would be worth more dead than alive — made Buffett his millions. But what made him his billions was buying the exact opposite of cigar butts — great franchises and great brands.

See's Candies holds a special place in Buffett-lore because of all the good that it had brought to Buffett's company, Berkshire Hathaway.

Buffett bought See's, a chocolate and candy manufacturer, for US$25 million back in 1972 and by 2003, had already earned a cumulative US$1 billion in pre-tax profits! That's an incredible 40,000% pre-tax return for Buffett over the years. The reason for such astonishing returns was because See's had an Economic Moat.

When See's Candies was purchased, Buffett had an important thought, *If we raised prices by 10 cents per pound, would sales fall off a cliff?* On hindsight, it would have been easy for us to say, *Of course not!* but at the time of purchase, Buffett was probably as confident about See's Candies ability to raise prices without losing business (a.k.a pricing power) as we are now — *without* the benefit of hindsight. In Buffett's mind, he figured that See's had 'mind share' wherever they sell their confectionaries. The public in California, USA, where See's predominantly does its business, associates the See's brand with quality gifts for their loved ones. This is how See's can maintain pricing power as people love the feel-good and 'loved-ones' associations with See's brand. This in essence is what an Economic Moat is all about — that which allows a business to earn above-average returns on capital over the long term by having pricing power.

There are actually signs within a business's numbers that can tell us if it possesses a Moat. Useful ones will include the presence of significant Free Cash Flow over the years and a good Return on Equity (usually meaning 15% or more) on an unlevered balance sheet. Do not be alarmed if you have no idea what all these terms mean — we will go through them in The Numbers. But for now, just take note of the fact that there can be numerical clues to point us toward businesses that might have an Economic Moat. But, it also pays to think about the qualitative aspects of the business to discern the presence of a moat. We would like to make it clear that a business with great financial figures need not necessarily have an Economic Moat and a business with a Moat *might* not have the best financial figures — when we invest we are trying to look for a combination of both.

Buffett likes an Economic Moat to the "body of water" protecting the "castle of out-sized profit". But, how do we identify if the "river" is present? This brings us to the factors that can tell us if an Economic Moat is present — and we'll have Pat Dorsey's excellent book *The Five Rules for Successful Stock Invseting* to thank in bringing us the framework for our thinking.

Product Differentiation

What makes the popular Gong Cha from Taiwan different from other bubble teas? The usual response would be that it tastes better from other brands of bubble teas; there is also the impression that Gong Cha's healthier because of the association with the Chinese character for "tea" in its namesake. This is actually product differentiation at work (we hope a light bulb goes on in your head!), similar to how Coca-Cola positions itself differently from other sodas, albeit on a smaller scale. Gong Cha tries to make its teas better-tasting than the rest of the competition to keep customers coming back.

Companies can differentiate their products by making it even better than competitors (such as having better specifications on smartphones) or making it *seem* better. Coca-Cola's sodas might not be exactly the tastiest and in blind taste tests, Pepsi-Cola does win out. But yet, Coke's market share of fizzy drink sales has consistently beaten that of Pepsi's. The reason is due to how Coke's brand is perceived by the general public. There is no need for Coke's product to actually be better along technical guidelines, as long as the people who are buying the drinks *feels* that it is better. All of this is due to Coke's relentless marketing to associate the drink with good and happy times — thus putting an association into people's minds about how 'good' Coke is every time they take a sip of it.

Even though a business can create a Moat purely by making better products, such moats can be transient. For example, when smartphones first started appearing in 2007, competitors to Apple's then-superior iPhone struggled to keep up with its technical specs. As time passed, competitors started getting better at the game and technical gaps between smartphones from different manufacturers started to narrow. Now, it can arguably be said that the smartphone manufacturers are playing on a level field with regard to the technical specs of their smartphones. Besides, there will always be a ceiling on how "good" a product can be before customers find that their experience with the product does not improve with the same quanta as the improvement in specs. When that happens, there can no longer be any meaningful differentiation in terms of better features or technology and the previously constructed Moat is gone.

Here, we would like to digress a little by saying that our example of the smartphone wars is not meant to say that Apple no longer has an Economic Moat. The subject of the presence or absence of a Moat for Apple is beyond the scope of this book. But, suffice it to say that the smartphone wars was used as an example of the dangers of building a Moat purely based on technological superiority. Now, back to the point...

In contrast, when customers *perceive* that a company's product is better, it can often be a much stronger and longer-lasting Moat. The evidence is in Coke's dominance over Pepsi and See's Candies' ability to raise prices consistently. No doubt, both companies have quality products within their circles of business, but it is the *brand* and all the positive associations that comes with it that gives Coke and See's Candies their enviable profitability.

Low Cost Producer

Imagine Companies A and B producing a non-differentiable widget as their main business. Company A is able to make the widget for $0.10

while Company B can only make the same widget for $0.50. Customers are only willing to buy the widgets at $0.60 per piece initially, so both companies can earn a profit and survive. But, what happens if customers now are only willing to pay $0.40 per widget? Eventually, Company B would not be able to absorb such losses and customers would migrate to Customer A, driving sales volume up to make up for the decrease in profit margin. Such is the power of the low-cost producer — the ability to stay in business when conditions sour, or the more obvious ability to price its products at prices lower than its next best competitor.

It can be easy to identify the presence of low costs — the gross, operating and net profit margins can tell us the story but it won't give us the full picture. We need to understand how a company achieves such cost efficiencies to gauge its sustainability. Usually, such efficiencies come about from two sources: better process and/or economies of scale.

Manufacturing companies are the ones commonly associated with economies of scale. Whatever gadgets or widgets that are being manufactured would require fixed capital investments — factories, equipment & software are some common examples. However, such fixed capital investments are usually volume-agnostic to a large degree, meaning it does not matter if you produce 10,000 units or 100,000 units — the amount you spend on these fixed investments would be largely similar. As a result, the Widget One, with 100,000 orders, would have a much smaller cost-per-unit than Widget Two with only 10,000 orders. This allows Widget One to undercut Widget Two's prices if Widget One wishes to do so (there might be times when anti-monopoly or anti-competitive laws would come into the picture, but it is beyond our scope of discussion here).

Microsoft is actually a great example of a company with huge economies of scale. The costs for developing software should be roughly in the same ballpark range for companies that want to create operating systems and work-station suites (such as Microsoft Office©).

After the relatively high development costs, which are 'fixed', the cost of transferring that information onto a CD or directly to the consumer through the internet 'cloud' is almost negligible. As a result, the overall cost-per-unit varies drastically depending on the quantity of soft-ware sold. If any company would like to compete with Microsoft, they would have to be able to tolerate extremely high cost-per-unit or have to capture significant market share in a short-time. Otherwise, Microsoft can easily charge lower prices (again, putting legal issues aside), making it tough for their competitors to continue with its business, owing to its extremely vast consumer-reach for their software.

High Switching Costs

Firms with high switching costs often make it very difficult and/or expensive for customers to switch out from their product or service and thus have the ability to charge their customers more and make more money. If you were the head of the IT department in a bank which has been using a suite of software from a specific vendor for all data processing functions, would you be inclined to switch to another vendor's software to save perhaps 10% on existing costs? The answer would most likely be no, because banks have operations that must go on for 24/7 and any switch in software would entail lengthy down-times which would cost the bank money. Furthermore, there are retraining costs to consider, which might not be explicitly captured in an income statement, but which exists nonetheless. All these are deterrents for the IT department to choose new software — hence, the existing vendor has built up a Moat due to high switching costs.

The American surgical-robot maker, Intuitive Surgical is a real-life example of how high switching costs has led to its success (the company's Net Income has grown from US$23.5 million in 2003 to US$495 million in 2011). Intuitive Surgical produces expensive surgical robots, called da Vinci robots, which are reported to be able to provide huge medical benefits for patients compared to traditional surgery (http://www.davincisurgery.com/). Training for the robot is not easy for the surgeon and it would be extremely time-consuming and difficult for the surgeon to switch to other types of surgical robots, if any, as the surgeon would have to undergo another difficult learning phase, even as he has to *continue* fulfilling his doctoral duties. The cost for each robot also goes up to the millions. It is not an easy investment for hospitals to make and so, once these robots are purchased, chances are they will not be replaced easily. We can see that Intuitive Surgical's Da Vinci robots make it both difficult *and* expensive (not just in monetary terms) for surgeons to switch to other competitor's products.

Computer-Aided-Design (CAD) software are great examples of a product with a high switching cost. CAD software are used in many different kinds of companies and some easy examples include architectural and engineering-design firms. If their engineers, architects and designers have already been trained in using AutoCAD®, which is developed and sold by AutoDesk Inc., there would be very little incentive to change the software unless a much, *much*, cheaper and easy-to-use alternative were to appear. CAD software often have a steep learning curve (notice the recurrence of a *learning curve* in products with high-switching cost? It's there for a reason) and there is also the issue of template-transfers. Imagine the years of design work that an engineering-design firm has saved in AutoCAD's file format which might not be readable with a competitor's product. In such a scenario, would the firm be enticed to switch to a different CAD software?

High Barriers to Entry

Often, the continued success of a business will attract the envy of others and competition ensues, eventually bringing profit margins for all participants down — that's the capitalist game. However, there are times when it is extremely difficult for competitors to enter an existing business to steal market share. Legal protection through patents and copyrights; regulatory protection; requirement of massive capital expenditures; and unassailable mind share are some examples of a high barrier to entry.

Patents and copyrights are commonly seen in the pharmaceutical and intellectual-property-heavy industries, such as video-gaming or movie making. In the USA, drug companies like Pfizer have patents over drugs that can last for years and during that time period, Pfizer gets to earn enormous profits from those drugs as competitors are prevented by patent laws from recreating the drugs. Disney holds the copyrights to iconic characters like Mickey Mouse and Disneyland and nobody would be able to use those characters to create cartoons, toys or films without the explicit permission of Disney. This allows *only* Disney to continue earning money from licensing these iconic cartoon characters for various commercial products.

A classic example of an unassailable mindshare would be Coke. We already discussed how Coke's products are favoured in our heads over all other sodas and that mental association is very hard, if not nearly impossible, to overcome. To that effect, Warren Buffett has said that *If you gave me $100 billion and said, 'Take away the soft-drink leadership of Coca-Cola in the world,' I'd give it back to you and say it can't be done.*

Network Effect

The Network Effect, in simple terms, is the way a product or service becomes more valuable as more people use it. A classic example of the Network Effect in action is the moat that credit card processors like Visa have created. Visa is so widely accepted by merchants worldwide because of the vast number of users of Visa cards *and* Visa cards are carried around by almost everybody because it is so widely accepted. If anyone where to compete with Visa, it has to setup a vast network of merchants and users very quickly and that is *very* tough to do so because no merchant would want to accept a card that is not widely used, while users would not see the value of carrying a card that is hardly accepted.

The Network Effect is also very pronounced on Social Media sites. Most people use Facebook (who doesn't!?) and realise the fact that it is very valuable because everyone else is using it — however, they fail to see the link between its value-because-everyone-is-using-it to an investing concept, which is a pity. Google's attempt at building a social media network through Google Plus is moving slower than the company would like to see because there aren't that many people using it, so what's the incentive for others to join the network?

Internet forums and chat-rooms actually display Network Effects as well, though they can be subtle. Motley Fool's (one of Ser Jing's favourite investing websites, by the way) community forums are actually very valuable because of the quantity and quality of its participants. These quality participants help to attract new participants, building an even stronger community.

If you can spot companies that have built a Moat because of the Network Effect, hang on to them tightly because Pat Dorsey views it as one of the strongest types of Moat.

Important Questions to ponder about...

1. Can you think of some businesses with strong economic moats?
2. What do you think creates their economic moat?
3. How durable is their moat? What are they doing to increase the durability of their moat?

Scuttlebutt

The business "grapevine" is a remarkable thing. It is amazing what an accurate picture of the relative points of strength and weakness of each

> *company in an industry can be obtained from a representative cross-section of the opinions of those who in one way or another are concerned with any particular company* — Philip Fisher

The term "scuttlebutt" was made famous by Philip Fisher in his book *Common Stocks and Uncommon Profits* which was first published in 1958. Scuttlebutt falls under the qualitative aspect of fundamental analysis.

Doing scuttlebutt means Prudent Investors talking to competitors, customers, suppliers, former employees (be wary of prejudiced comments), management of company and current employees. By talking to these people, one can determine if the company is a good buy. Scuttlebutting also involves using one's observational skills to look at businesses.

In his book, Philip mentioned the following:

> *It is amazing what an accurate picture of the relative points of strength and weakness of each company in an industry can be obtained from a representative cross-section of the opinions of those who in one way or another are concerned with any particular company. Most people, particularly if they feel sure there is no danger of their being quoted, like to talk about the field of work in which they are engaged and will talk rather freely about their competitors. Go to five companies in an industry, ask each of them intelligent questions about the points of strength and weakness of the other four, and nine times out of ten a surprisingly detailed and accurate picture of all five will emerge.*
>
> *It is equally astonishing how much can be learned from both vendors and customers about the real nature of the people with whom they deal. Research scientists in universities, in government, and in competitive companies are another fertile source of worthwhile data. So are executives of trade associations* — Philip Fisher

For instance, if you are researching into a Food and Beverage (F&B) company, you can visit the restaurant and see if it is being patronized regularly, especially during non-peak hours. You can talk to the customers and ask them why they like visiting this particular restaurant. You can also talk to the staff there to understand the company culture and why they like/do not like working in the company.

Therefore, scuttlebutt is basically going the extra mile to find out more information about the company that may not be found through conventional means — reading the annual reports and analyst reports, pouring through websites, forums and SGX company announcements. Be creative in your scuttlebutting and you may uncover certain aspects of the business that not many know of!

Important Questions to ponder about…

1. How do you think scuttlebutt can fit into your investment process?
2. What other methods of scuttlebutt can you think of?
3. How does scuttlebutt give the retail investor an edge over the professional or institutional investors?

Reading an Annual Report

Other guys read Playboy. *I read annual reports*

— Warren Buffett

A company's annual report is akin to the report card of a student. As Prudent Investors, we should learn to love to read the annual report. Many investors chuck aside the annual report as they find it a bore. The annual report provides a "one-stop shop" for investors to learn more about the company they are interested in and gives a treasure trove of information. The annual report details information of the company such as the business the company is involved in, the management team and the financial statements of the company, among others. The reason many shareholders chuck aside the annual report once they receive them is that they do not understand how to read the annual report. They also fail to understand that reading the annual report allows them to make informed decisions about the company. In this section, we hope we can make you love reading the annual report. If tonight, after reading this section, you feel like hugging the annual report to sleep, we have done an exceptional job!

Potential investors of a company can obtain the annual report online through the company website, SGX website or by simply emailing the Investor Relations (IR) department to send you a copy of the annual report. Most IR department will be more than willing to send you a copy of the annual report. However, nowadays, many blue-chip companies are moving away from printing physical copies for sustainability issues. They only provide digital versions of the annual report which can be downloaded easily from the sources mentioned above.

The annual report is released after each financial year and it is mandatory for listed companies in Singapore to provide the annual report for its shareholders at least 14 days before the date of the Annual General Meeting. The rules governing the release of annual reports are stipulated in the SGX Rulebook, Chapter 7, Part III.

The following information will be contained in a typical annual report of a company:

- Corporate Profile
- Financial Highlights
- Chairman's Statement
- Operations Review
- Board of Directors and Key Management
- Corporate Information
- Corporate Governance Report
- Report of the Directors
- Statement by Directors
- Independent Auditors' Report
- Financial Statements
    - Consolidated Income Statement
    - Consolidated Statement of Comprehensive Income
    - Balance Sheets
    - Statements of Changes in Equity
    - Consolidated Statement of Cash Flows
- Notes to Financial Statements
- Statistics of Shareholders
- Notice of Annual General Meeting
- Proxy Form

Some of the terms above may vary among different annual reports but the basic information provided will be the same among all companies.

Corporate Profile and Financial Highlights

The corporate profile, as the name suggests, shows the business the company is involved in and the various divisions and segments of the business. It also shows the various countries the business has offices in.

The financial highlights of the company provide a graphical format of the company's past key financial metrics such as the revenue, profit, earnings per share, current ratio, dividends paid out, return on equity, among others (fret not, the terms mentioned above will be covered under "The Numbers" part of the book later). The financial highlights allow investors to see how well the company has done over the past few years.

Chairman's Statement

One of the most important aspects of the annual report is the Chairman's Statement. In this statement, the Chief Executive Officer (CEO) or the Chairman (or both have their own statements depending on the company), divulges what the company has done over the past financial year, the accomplishments and challenges faced and what are the future plans of the company. Ensure that the Chairman talks about how the challenges the company faced were overcome. Some CEOs provide their own take of the industry prospects and whether the year ahead will be challenging.

Most CEOs or Chairmen will try to paint a rosy picture of the company as they are "selling" the company to potential investors. Therefore, Prudent Investors should not take whatever that is mentioned in the statement at face value. They should investigate the statement in-depth.

The statement also allows investors to know if the management is honest and forthcoming. If a mistake was done over the past year, the statement should acknowledge the mistake and accept that the management "screwed it up" instead of glossing over the mistake. Some companies that are not doing well financially may even be skimpy on the details so do look out for such red flags.

It is paramount that Prudent Investors read at least the past five years of Chairman's Statements to look out for consistency and if the plans put out previously are still on track. Reading past statements also allows investors to know whether the company has delivered on its promises or if the company is just an empty vessel making a lot of noise. For example, if in 2006, the company you are looking into has said that it will expand into China by 2011, make sure that the company has kept its word and has really ventured into China. If it has not done so, query why not as the company might be trying to sweep things under the carpet and hoping no one notices. Also, note if there is any change in the tone of the statements over the past years. Has it become more optimistic or pessimistic?

To hone the skills of reading between the lines of a Chairman's Statement, investors can read the Chairman's Statements of various companies, especially those of loss-making companies. By comparing the tone and forthrightness among the various Chairman's Statements, investors can become more prudent and easily sieve out the good companies from the bad ones. Or, you can check out an excellent book for investors on how to discern quality corporate communication from L.J. Rittenhouse called *Investing Between the Lines* (it was recommended by Buffett too!).

Operations Review

This part of the annual report shows how the various divisions of the company fared over the past financial year. This section lets you understand more about the company and how it makes money.

If after looking into the corporate profile, financial highlights, the Chairman's Statement and the operation review, you do not get a good feel of the company or do not understand how the company makes money, it is better to pass on this company. There are so many other companies out there that are worth your time and money.

Board of Directors and Key Management

This section shows the profile of various directors and key managers of the business. The board of directors usually consists of the Chairman, Managing Director, Executive Directors, Vice-Chairman, Non-Executive Directors and Independent Directors. The key management usually consists of the general managers, Chief Financial Officer and Chief Executive Officer.

Corporate Governance Report

This part of the annual report shows the number of board meetings held for the past year and the attendance, date of appointments and date of last re-election of the directors, remuneration of the directors and top executives of the company, among others.

The most important part of this section is the remuneration of the top echelon of the company. Prudent Investors should scrutinize the remuneration packages and ensure the directors are not overly compensated. This can be done by comparing the remuneration between the various companies in the same industry. Compensation package for the company you are looking into should be around the same region as the other companies.

Report of the Directors, Statement of Directors and Independent Auditors' Report

The Report of the Directors consists of the direct and deemed interest in shares of the directors of the company. The Statement of Directors is simply a statement by the directors saying that the financial statements to be presented in the annual report are true.

The Independent Auditors' Report states that the financial statements have been audited and are in accordance to the standards. Prudent Investors should make sure the auditors are not changing hands frequently. If that is the case, it could be a strong indication of troubles ahead.

Financial Statements

This is another important part of the annual report. The three main sections of the financial statements that Prudent Investors look at are the Consolidated Income Statement, Balance Sheets and Consolidated Statement of Cash Flows. The Consolidated Statement of Comprehensive Income and Statements of Changes in Equity are not that important, as they are not really financial statements but more of supporting schedules. In the later part of the book, we will show you how to read the financial statements in-depth.

Notes to Financial Statements

This part follows the financial statements. It provides a detailed explanation of how some of the figures in the financial statements were obtained. It forms an integral part of the financial statements and should be read together.

Statistics of Shareholders, Notice of Annual General Meeting and Proxy Form

The Statistics of Shareholders shows the number of issued shares, class of shares and the voting rights. It also shows a list of the substantial shareholders of the company. By looking at this list, Prudent Investors can know if management holds a significant portion of the outstanding shares.

The Notice of Annual General Meeting (AGM) lets shareholders know when and where the upcoming AGM will be held and the resolutions to be passed. The Proxy Form is for shareholders to appoint another party to attend the AGM on his/her behalf.

This brings us to an end for the Story — all the squishy and sometimes hard-to-quantify factors of a company that can help to determine whether it will make a good investment. But like we mentioned earlier, the Story cannot come without the Numbers and vice versa. Thus, we will now like to embark on a study of the Numbers. It will be fun — or so we hope!

Important Questions to ponder about…

1. How useful is an annual report in helping you learn more about the business?
2. What are the important aspects of an annual report you should look out for?
3. How do you discern if the Chairman's Statement is truthful?

The Numbers

> *Not everything that can be counted counts, and not everything that counts can be counted* — Albert Einstein

If you recall, we mentioned earlier that Prudent Investing involves The Story, The Numbers and The Mind. We have just covered The Story and would now like to talk about The Numbers. Ser Jing likes to say that *You can't have the Story without the Numbers, and the Numbers without the Story* — both have to exist for an investment to be considered a prudent choice.

Under The Numbers, there are three sub-sections. The first would deal with Financial Statement Analysis where we would give some notes on how you can read a financial statement and hopefully not bore you to sleep in the process. The second would be more exciting and would deal with Valuation methods, where we would present some methods to arrive at an *estimate* of the intrinsic value of a business with which we can make our investment decisions. Lastly, we would talk about Margin of Safety — a concept with which we can use to minimise risk of capital loss in our investments.

Financial Statement Analysis

Reading Financial Statements

When trying to understand a business, it is of great importance that you know how to look at Financial Statements — statements prepared by companies and their auditors that convey the state of their business. Investing in stocks without knowing the financial statements would be akin to buying a house without caring about how much you are paying for the housing loan — a dangerous situation for most people! In this section, we will refer to the financial statements of the fictional XYZ Corporation in Pages lxiii–lxv to help you understand financial statements. Take note that financial institutions such as insurance companies and banks, as well as some public utilities have financial statements that are different from XYZ Corporation's financial statements. For most other businesses, the financial statements will look very similar to the ones we are going to discuss soon.

There are three financial statements that every publicly-listed company has to showcase, and they are, (1) the Income Statement, (2) Cash Flow Statement, and (3) Balance Sheet.

(1) **Summary of the Income Statement**: The Income Statement, also known as the Profit and Loss Statement (P&L Statement), records the sales made by the business over a period of time and deducts all the relevant expenses to arrive at the Net Income figure. Since most publicly traded companies have to file quarterly reports every three months and an annual report at the end of their financial year, the Income Statement usually encompasses the sales and expenses for three months as well as one financial year.

It is also known as the "profit and loss statement" or "statement of revenue and expense."

Investors find the section on operating items most interesting because it discloses information about the revenues and expenses of the business.

The non-operating items section deals with activities that are not directly related to a company's regular operations.

(2) **Summary of the Cash Flow Statement:** The Cash Flow Statement records the actual amount of cash that is flowing into and out of the business over a period of time. Cash is the lifeblood of a business and the Cash Flow Statement records how much cash is used up and produced by the business for different purposes.

The cash positions of public companies may not be reflected on the Income Statement due to accrual accounting, hence, it would be prudent to check the Cash Flow Statement to see if the company is having problems with its cashflow management.

For example, the company might have clinched a million dollar deal which is recognized as revenue on the Income Statement, however, the company has yet to receive the cash from the deal until a much later date.

The key here is for investors to check if the company has been managing its cashflow prudently.

(3) **Summary of the Balance Sheet:** In the simplest of terms, the Balance Sheet records what a business owns (Assets) and owes (Liabilities) and tell us the financial condition of the business. It is important to know what are the Assets and Liabilities that a business has to ascertain the business's health. As an individual, we would like to know what we own as well as how much money we owe. It is the same case for a business. Like an individual, owing other parties too much money is not a good thing, and that is generally true for most businesses.

It is important to note that different countries will have different accounting reporting standards. For example, in Singapore, companies use the International Financial Reporting Standards (IFRS) which are then modified to suit each country's unique needs. Some other countries that have adopted the IFRS include Australia, Canada, the European Union and Japan. The USA is currently using Generally Accepted Accounting Principles (GAAP), which is different from IFRS. However, the differences between these accounting standards are beyond the scope of this book and we think most investors should not be too hung up over the intricacies of accounting either. An understanding of what Financial Statements mean and how the numbers can help unearth good investment ideas is what is important.

We've given a basic summary of what each Financial Statement means. For those of you who are keen to run through each line item found in the financial statements to allow you to have an understanding of what they mean and eventually, how they all come together to help you find great businesses to invest in, please refer to the Appendix.

Valuation

> *The stock market is filled with individuals who know the price of everything, but the value of nothing*
>
> — Phillip Fisher

Warren Buffett often talks about comparing his own *estimate* of the Intrinsic Value of a business against its stock price when he is making a decision on whether to purchase shares or acquire the whole business itself. As a brief refresher, please bear in mind that for any business that is listed on a stock exchange, there may come times when its Intrinsic Value is (1) a lot lower than its share price, (2) a lot higher than its share price and (3) roughly equal to its share price. As an investor, we would ideally love to buy at (1) and sell at (2).

Put simply, Intrinsic Value is an *estimate* of the true worth of a business to an investor, which is distinct from its stock price. There are two common ways to calculate the Intrinsic Value of a business, and they involve the use of Relative Valuation or a Discounted Cash Flow Model. Now, before we delve into the fuzzy-land of growth projections and estimates, there is a phrase you *have* to remember when it comes to valuation techniques — **G**arbage **I**n, **G**arbage **O**ut (**GIGO**). Please repeat this phrase after us, "GIGO, GIGO, and GIGO!" Done? Great! What this phrase means is that the accuracy and quality of the output of our valuation technique is entirely dependent on the quality of the assumptions and estimates we make for the inputs. Over the next few pages, you will come to see just how powerful a small change in inputs can be in affecting the final valuation figure. So, please bear in mind **GIGO** and with this powerful phrase, we shall proceed further into fuzzy-land (in a step-by-step manner) with you and try to come up with an *estimate* of the Intrinsic Value of XYZ Corporation based upon their Financial Statements found on Pages lxiii–lxv.

Compounded Annual Growth Rate

Let us digress to two very important points before we begin with our valuation methods. The first important point concerns a mathematical term that you have to understand in order for you to understand the valuation methods we are working with — the Compounded Annual Growth Rate (CAGR). The formula needed to calculate a CAGR is the most complicated formula you will encounter in this book. However, it only requires secondary school mathematics — and no algebra or calculus is needed, we promise!

The CAGR is similar in concept to the *compound* interest that your bank pays you in a savings account. For example, imagine a bank that pays you 5% compound interest per year. At the start of the first year, you deposited $1000 with the bank. At the end of the first year you will get $50 in interest and your bank account is now worth $1050. At the end of the second year, you will be getting 5% of $1050 in interest, and your bank account is now worth $1102.50. At the end of the third year, you will be getting 5% of $1102.50 in interest and your account is now worth $1157.625 and so on and so forth. The table below shows how your bank account will look like after 10 years at 5% compound interest.

Start of Year	Account Balance at 5% Compound Interest
1	$1000.00
2	$1050.00
3	$1102.50
4	$1157.63
5	$1215.51
6	$1276.28
7	$1340.10
8	$1407.10
9	$1477.46
10	$1551.33

With the starting amount and the compound interest, we can know the end amount we require after a certain time. For the calculation of a CAGR, the known figures are the starting amount, end amount and time span. We want to calculate a hypothetical "compound interest" figure that can be applied to the same starting amount and arrive at the same end amount given the same time span.

Without going into too many mathematical details, the formula for CAGR actually looks like this:

$$\text{CAGR} = [(\text{End Amount} / \text{Starting Amount})^{1/n} - 1] \times 100\%,$$
$$\text{where } n = \text{Number of Years}$$

If we use the imagined bank account as an example, the relevant figures are given as follows:

$$\text{End Amount} = \$1551.33$$
$$\text{Starting Amount} = \$1000$$
$$n = 9$$

So, let us plug in the numbers into our formula:

$$\text{CAGR} = [(\$1551.33/\$1000)^{1/9} - 1] \times 100\% = 5\%$$

This is all there is to it for understanding what is the CAGR.

Price-Earnings Multiple

The next important point we want to discuss is the concept of the Price Earnings multiple, or PE multiple. We mentioned earlier that the EPS figure is one of the most widely used figures in financial media and it is because EPS is an essential component in calculating the PE multiple of any business that is publicly-listed.

$$PE = \text{Price Per Share} / EPS$$

The PE multiple accorded to any publicly-listed company by the market is affected by a myriad of factors such as; the market's sentiment toward the future growth in a company's earnings, the quality of their management, historical earnings growth rate of a company, general economic conditions, etc. However, a good way to think about an "appropriate" PE multiple for a company would be a value that is in-line with its estimated future growth in earnings.

The PE multiple is essentially the premium that an investor pays for each dollar of earnings. If an investor is paying a PE multiple of 30 for a business that has an EPS of $1, the investor is paying $30 for every $1 of the business's earnings. Perhaps, the investor is anticipating explosive growth in the business's earnings for many years ahead or perhaps the business has really stable revenues and earnings such that investors are willing to pay a premium for the stability that the business brings. The PE multiple awarded to companies by the market is essentially affected by investor sentiment toward all aspects of the business — its earnings, its management, its line of business, its industry, its future growth path and so on and so forth.

This is one of the reasons why a business that has an earnings growth rate higher than its PE multiple can often be great investment opportunities because there is a good chance the market might award the business with a higher PE multiple and so an investor in the business can benefit from both earnings growth as well as a higher PE multiple (a process known as "multiple expansion"). Shelby Davis had a really cool name for it — he called it the "Davis Double Play". A simple table below that was shown in John Neff's *John Neff on Investing* is reproduced below to illustrate the point.

Current Market Price	Static PE	Expanded PE
Current earnings per share	$2.00	$2.00
Current market price	$26	$16
Current PE multiple	13	8
Growth Rate	11%	11%
Expected Earnings	$2.22	$2.22
New PE multiple	13	11
New Market Price	$28.86	$24.42
Appreciation potential	**11%**	**53%**

Now that you have gained an understanding of what CAGR is and how a PE multiple can affect an investment, let us take a look at the Meat of this section — our Valuation Methods!

Relative Valuation

Why is this method called Relative Valuation? The answer lies in the fact that we are trying to normalise all share prices so that we have a basis for comparison. Take for example, one share of Company A that is selling at $50 and one share of Company B that is selling at $5. At face value, Company A's share is more expensive than Company B's share because it costs $45 more per share. But, we know that each share represents a small slice of a company and that by buying a share, we are buying a small piece of everything the company owns and owes. Thus, we need a basis of comparison to make a decision on what is expensive or cheap.

Because of this, we need to divide the share price of a company with the value of "something" that is embedded within each share. This "something" can be the company's earnings, revenue, operating cash flow, net asset value, kitchen sink, car tyre — anything! What this means is that, all of a sudden, we can compare two companies on an equal basis and see which is really more expensive.

Let's assume here that we want to have a comparison on the basis of a company's earnings, sales, free cash flow and book value. The relevant figures for Company A and B are given in the table below:

	Company A	Company B
Earnings Per Share	$10	$0.05
Sales Per Share	$50	$1
Free Cash Flow Per Share	$15	$0.075
Book Value Per Share	$20	$1.5

If we divide the Price Per Share by the different financial figures, we would obtain:

(1) Price Per Share / Earnings Per Share = Price Earnings multiple (PE)
(2) Price Per Share / Sales Per Share = Price-to-Sales multiple (PS)
(3) Price Per Share / Free Cash Flow Per Share = Price-to-Free Cash Flow multiple (PFCF)
(4) Price Per Share / Book Value Per Share = Price-to-Book (PB)

And now we have Company A and Company B on an equal basis for comparison:

	Company A	Company B
PE	5	100
PS	1	5
PFCF	3.33	66.67
PB	2.5	3.33

From the table above, putting all qualitative factors aside, we can now see that Company B looks a lot more expensive than Company A based on PE, PS, PFCF and PB even though Company B's share price is cheaper on an absolute basis. This is what Relative Valuation can do — it can help us compare the "pricey-ness" of different companies' shares.

And what are trying to do, is to use Relative Valuation to help us find an estimate of Intrinsic Value of a company using its PE multiple. Let's get started!

(1) **Calculate the historical Compounded Annual Growth Rate (CAGR) in Net Income of the business over at least five years**

Do bear in mind that if the starting point for those five years happened to be part of an economic recession, it would be better to extend the number of years' of data to at least two years *before* the onset of the recession. This is done to offset any distorting effects that might occur due to an unusually low starting point for Net Income as a consequence of economic recessions, which would artificially inflate the CAGR figure.

If we take a look at the Income Statement for XYZ Corporation on Pages lxiii–lxv, we see that we only have data extending to Fiscal Year (FY) 2008 and while we know that the most recent global financial crisis that affected the world's economy happened in 2007–2009, we can only make do with the data we have. So, let us use 2008 as a starting point. Using the formula for CAGR given earlier, we can compute the historical CAGR figure for Net Income to be:

End Amount: $4,484,000 (Net Income in 2012)
Starting Amount: $900,000 (Net Income in 2008)
$n = 4$
CAGR = $[(\$4484000/\$900000)^{1/4} - 1] \times 100\%$ = **49.4%**

(2) **Calculate the historical CAGR in Average No. of Diluted Shares Outstanding over the same time period as you use for Net Income**

We need this figure because we can then use this as a rough-gauge for the kind of shareholder dilution that might occur. The reason for choosing the same time-frame as that used in Step 1 is purely for convenience purposes.

From the Income Statement of XYZ Corporation, we can see that the diluted share count has not increased, so it is obvious that the CAGR would be 0%. In such cases, it would be perfectly logical to stick with 0% for use in further steps.

(3) **Use the historical CAGR of Net Income found in Step 1 as a guide, along with the qualitative aspects of the business, to come up with an informed estimate of future growth rates for the next five years**

This is where things get really fuzzy. Humans are actually pretty bad at predicting the future (more on that later, in The Mind) and so, when we try to come up with a figure like future growth rates, it is always best to *err on the side of caution.*

From Step (1), XYZ Corporation has had historical CAGR of 49.4% since 2008 — that is an extremely high rate of growth. It is seldom the case where there are companies that can grow Net Income at such rates sustainably. XYZ Corporation operates coffee-shops. Coffee is a staple drink in the morning for a large portion of the population. Thus, it would be logical to think that XYZ Corporation's business is not a fad, but rather a business that has staying power and one in which growth can continue if they open more coffee shops.

Because of the factors listed above, it would be *prudent* to dial back our estimates of future growth to be around 20–25% over the next five years (do note that an earnings growth rate of 20–25% per annum is *fantastic*!). Let us use **20%** as a round number for easier computation. Remember, Intrinsic Value is an *estimate* and like Warren Buffett says *It is better to be approximately right than precisely wrong* — we only have to have a rough estimate of Intrinsic Value for us to find good investments.

(4) **Use the historical CAGR of Average No. of Diluted Shares Outstanding found in Step 2 as a guide to come up with an informed estimate of future No. of Diluted Shares Outstanding for the next five years**

Since XYZ Corporation's diluted share count remained unchanged from 2008 to 2012, we can safely assume that share count will either remain constant or grow by a very small amount over the next five years. Because of that, we can assume that the average diluted share count for XYZ Corporation in five years' time will be 10,000,000.

(5) **Use the estimated growth rate, the most current Net Income figure and the estimated diluted share count to come up with an estimated EPS figure five years from now**

We now know that Net Income for XYZ Corporation in 2012 was \$4.484 million. We also know that its estimated growth rate would be 20% for the next five years while its CAGR for average diluted share count has been 0%. Using the information we have, we are then able to come up with our estimates on the EPS of XYZ Corporation in five years.

EPS in 5 years = [Net Income in 2012 × (Future Growth Rate + 1)^N]/Average No. of Diluted Shares Outstanding, where N = number of years

So, if we plug in the relevant numbers, our equation is going to look like this:

EPS in 5 years = [\$4,484,000 × (1 + 0.20)^5]/10,000,000 = **\$1.12**

(6) **Multiply the calculated EPS in Step 5 with an appropriate PE Multiple to arrive at an *estimated* share price in five years' time**

Remember that we mentioned earlier that an "appropriate" way to think about the PE multiple would be for it to be the same value as the business's estimated future growth rate. We had come up with a Net Income growth rate of 20% for XYZ Corporation based upon quantitative as well as qualitative factors and so an immediate response might be to place a PE multiple of 20.

However, things are not always that simple. Maybe XYZ Corporation's growth might slow at the end of the fifth year? Perhaps XYZ Corporation's management becomes even more highly regarded by the public or perhaps a new scientific study might be released in the future which shows that coffee is (gasp!) health-destroying? All these factors can affect the PE multiple associated with a business in both good and bad ways and so, it is always better to come up with a range for the PE multiple that you expect the shares of the business to sport.

Without diving into the details, let's just accept that a PE multiple of 15–25 is acceptable for XYZ Corporation Thus, based upon all our calculations from Step 1 to Step 6, a likely share price of XYZ Corporation in five years' time is given as

Likely Share Price in Five Years' Time = PE Multiple × EPS
= (15 to 25) × \$1.12
= **\$16.8 to \$28**

(7) **Discount the share price calculated in Step 6 at your desired Discount Rate back to the present to arrive at Intrinsic Value**

This is the final step required in calculating an Intrinsic Value of a business using the Relative Valuation method. In Step 6, we arrived at a share price that XYZ Corporation might display five years from now. However, we also need to know a suitable share price for us to buy *now* if we want to achieve a certain annual rate of return on our investment from now till five years later. Thus, we will need to discount the calculated share price in Step 6 back to the present.

Some good suggestions for the discount rate could be 15% (because if the share price of the company can grow at 15% per year, it will double within five years) or a benchmark you will hope to beat, such as the CPF interest of 4%. This is also known as your hurdle rate — the rate at which you hope your investment's growth can "hurdle" over. Do note that if your discount rate is too high, everything will look unbelievably expensive to you and if your discount rate is too low, everything will look unbelievably cheap to you instead. Ultimately, it boils down to your own personal choice. However, let's assume that you had picked 15% to be your discount rate. Thus, if we discount the share price found in Step 6 by 15% per annum back to the present, we would see figures such as:

Intrinsic Value = (Share Price in Five Years)/(1 + Discount Rate^N, where N = number of years

Intrinsic Value = (\$16.8 to \$28) / $(1 + 0.15)^5$ = **\$8.35 to \$13.92**

So, ultimately, we have arrived at an Intrinsic Value of \$8.35 to \$13.92 for each share of XYZ Corporation based upon a Relative Valuation method whereupon we calculated EPS growth of a business, tagged a PE multiple to the EPS to arrive at an estimated share price in a few years' time before we finally discount the estimated share price back to the present. If our calculated Intrinsic Value of a business is actually higher than its current share price, than we would know that a business is under-valued and it would be a suitable candidate for investment.

Now you have a new tool-kit you can use in your Investing Tool-Box when you are analysing companies! However, there is something really important we would want to show you before we move on to the next valuation technique.

Let us go back to Step 5 and use a slightly different figure for future growth instead — let's use 22% instead of 20%. That would result in an EPS of \$1.22. Now, let us go to Step 6 and apply a PE multiple of 30 instead of 15–25. That would result in a share price of \$36.6. If we follow the same discount rate used in Step 7, we would arrive at an Intrinsic Value of \$18.20 instead. That is 2.18 times more than the low end of our initial Intrinsic Value estimate! The reason for this exercise is to highlight how sensitive Intrinsic Value calculations can be because of slight changes to our inputs — remember GIGO? Thus, there is always this danger that we might easily knead the numbers until the share price of a particular company appears under-valued *because we have already had this notion that we want to purchase this company's shares for investment.* Aswath Damodaran, Finance Professor from New York University's Stern School of Business mentioned in his lectures that *People decide what they want to pay. Then they look for the justification.* So, we would like to implore you to please try and be as brutally honest as possible toward yourself when performing valuation of businesses, be it using the Relative Valuation method, or the Discounted Cash Flow method.

A summary of the seven steps involved in coming up with an Intrinsic Value estimate using the Relative Valuation method is given as follows:

(1) Calculate the historical Compounded Annual Growth Rate (CAGR) in Net Income of the business over at least five years.
(2) Calculate the historical CAGR in Average No. of Diluted Shares Outstanding over the same time period as you use for Net Income.
(3) Use the historical CAGR of Net Income found in Step 1 as a guide, along with the qualitative aspects of the business, to come up with an informed estimate of future growth rates for the next five years.
(4) Use the historical CAGR of Average No. of Diluted Shares Outstanding found in Step 2 as a guide to come up with an informed estimate of future No. of Diluted Shares Outstanding for the next five years.
(5) Use the estimated growth rate, the most current Net Income figure and the estimated diluted share count to come up with an estimated EPS figure five years from now.
(6) Multiply the calculated EPS in Step 5 with an appropriate PE Multiple to arrive at an estimated share price in five years' time.
(7) Discount the share price calculated in Step 6 at your desired Discount Rate back to the present to arrive at Intrinsic Value.

Discounted Cash Flow Model

The Discounted Cash Flow (DCF) model is the most commonly taught valuation method in Business Schools, and is also considered the more rigorous method for Intrinsic Value calculation. However, what we are going to go through would be a watered-down version that is less *precise* but no less *useful* by any means. Precision is over-rated in the world of finance and extremely precise models usually only adds to the *confidence* that the model-ler has about the model but the accuracy of it is not necessarily improved by the added precision (this is an important concept in Behavioural Psychology which will be explored later in The Mind). Aswath Damodaran made a joke in one of his lectures about the use of false-precision by finance professionals, *When in doubt, use Decimals!*. Regarding this, we would add, *When in doubt, use Caution!* As Albert Einstein says *Make everything as Simple as possible, but not Simpler* — when it comes to Investing, we really like to **K**eep **I**t **S**imple, **S**tupid (KISS)!

The DCF Model is essentially used to try and calculate all the cash that can be extracted from a business for its shareholders. What we would try to do is to analyse the Cash Flow statement of a business and come up with an estimate of how Free Cash Flow (gosh, not another estimation *again*!?) would look like for the business from now till Kingdom Come. Then, we would discount all that future Free Cash Flow back into the present and add them all up to form our Intrinsic Value estimate for the business. It might sound complicated, but it really is quite simple when we break it down into a few simple steps.

Free Cash Flow is used in the DCF Model because it is the residual cash from Operating Cash Flow that is left-over after the company has invested in assets that it requires to maintain its business. We mentioned earlier that Free Cash Flow can be used for acquisitions for growth, repurchasing of shares and to pay out dividends to shareholders without resorting to borrowing money or issuing more shares for capital and is ultimately the cash that can be extracted from the business for the benefit of shareholders. The formula for Free Cash Flow is reproduced below for your convenience.

Free Cash Flow = Operating Cash Flow – Purchase of Property, Plant and Equipment

There are no new mathematical concepts we have to go through for use in a DCF Model even though there is a caveat to be noted when using it — it is a model that is extremely difficult to apply to cyclical companies. Cyclical companies' revenue, earnings and cash flow increase and decrease violently, amplifying the more gentle swings of the economic cycle. A DCF model would be more useful in the context of companies with more stable businesses — businesses whose results do not fluctuate wildly with economic cycles.

Before we begin with a step-by-step breakdown of a Discounted Cash Flow valuation, here is the formula for using a Discounted Cash Flow:

(1) **Calculate the historical CAGR of Free Cash Flow for the business over the last five years**

The premise behind the choice of a suitable starting point for our calculation of the historical CAGR of Free Cash Flow would be exactly the same as that of Step 1 in the Relative Valuation section. From XYZ Corporation's Cash Flow statements we can see that Free Cash Flow has increased from $990,000 in FY2008 to $2,404,000 in FY2012. If we plug in the relevant numbers into our formula for CAGR, we would obtain:

End Amount: $2,404,000 (Free Cash Flow in 2012)
Starting Amount: $990,000 (Free Cash Flow in 2008)
$n = 4$
CAGR = $[(\$2404000/\$990006)^{1/4} - 1] \times 100\% =$ **24.8%**

(2) **Estimate the future growth rates of Free Cash Flow. Use the historical CAGR of Free Cash Flow together with the qualitative aspects of the business to come up with an estimate for the high-growth rate**

A DCF Model usually encompasses a few periods of different growth rates for the business that the model is being used on. For example, you might model 20% growth for three years, followed by 10% growth for another three years and then 3% growth to perpetuity. The reason for doing so is to try and incorporate an element of conservatism into our estimates of growth because we, as humans, are generally pretty horrible with a crystal ball (humans are generally pretty lousy at making predictions, a concept which we will explore in greater detail in The Mind)

We would like to add a disclaimer here that estimating the growth rate for Free Cash Flow using the Cash Flow statement might not really be academically acceptable. Very rigorous approaches (not uncommon in academia or investment banks) might even make use of forecasts of each line item in the Income Statement and Balance Sheet to come up with the Cash Flow Statement but therein lies the problem. If we already know we are so bad at forecasting, we should *minimise* the amount of forecasting needed in any of our analytical work with regard to investment valuations — thus, our preference for a simple definition of Free Cash Flow and an almost fuss-free way of estimating its future growth.

There are really no hard and fast rules with regard to how many different growth "steps" and the time-width of each step that you want to incorporate into your model. What is more important here is that you use your understanding of the qualitative aspects of the business as well as the historical CAGR calculated in Step 1 to come up with growth estimates that *appeal to your common sense.* So for example, we might think that XYZ Corporation will have five years of Free Cash Flow growth in the region of 20%, before growth is halved in the next five years to 10%. Theoretically, we are supposed to come up with "precise" growth estimates for a business for as long as we *think* we can foresee into the future. Practically, we think it is a little ridiculous to look 50–100 years ahead for precise growth estimates. As such (and as is always the case) we want to be conservative and so precise estimates for growth are usually given for around 10 years or less.

Beyond that, the next step would be to estimate a terminal growth rate for a business, which is the rate at which the business would grow at perpetually. The terminal growth rate is usually assumed to be the long-term growth rate of a stable economy. The implication behind this assumption is that if the business's long-term growth rate was larger than even a country's economic growth, the business would soon become *the* economy of a country itself and as it continues growing, it would soon take over the world's economic output and eventually that of the galaxy itself! We're not too sure about you, but the notion of a business being the entire world's economy seems a *tad* far-fetched and so we would like to stick with a terminal growth that is in-line with a stable economy's long-term growth rate. We can look at the long-term growth rate of the Scandinavian countries, Switzerland, USA or even our own little red dot as a form of guidance. In this instance, we think 3% would make a logical choice for the terminal growth rate.

So, the growth figures we have chosen to use for XYZ Corporation are: **20%** for five years, **10%** for the next five years, and **3%** for the perpetual growth figure.

(3) **Choose a suitable Discount Rate which will be used to discount all the Future Cash Flows back into the present. Calculate the Discounted Future Cash Flows using the Formula given earlier**

The very name of the DCF Model should signal the fact that a Discount Rate is going to be involved sooner or later. Theoretically, the Discount Rate that is normally used is the summation of what is termed the Risk-Free Rate of return and the Equity Risk Premium. Simply defined, the Equity Risk Premium encompasses the additional return that investors require for bearing the risk of investing in equities (a.k.a stocks). It's a lengthy discussion about what the Equity Risk Premium actually entails and is beyond the scope of this book.

Instead of using the 'normally-accepted' Discount Rate definition, an equally valid way would be to choose a hurdle rate (and it is our preferred method), just as we have done in Step 7 of the Relative Valuation model. Let us stick to 15% so that we can have an equal basis for comparison between our estimates of XYZ Corporation's Intrinsic Value using the two different methods. Thus, a Discount Rate of **15%** is chosen.

(4) **Use the estimated growth rates for Free Cash Flow and the Discount Rate for use in the Discounted Cash Flow model**

Before we touch on the formulas needed to get our Discounted Cash Flow model to work, we would like to expound a little on the idea of "Present Value of Future Cash Flows". Aesop describes the idea succinctly with his quote, *A bird in the hand is worth two in the bush.* We should almost always *never* pay more in the present for a future cash flow. For example, if we were to promise you a $1000 cash payment that would be made 10 years from now, how much are you willing to pay us for this $1000 cash payment?

A logical thing to do would be to think of the best investment you know you can safely make and use those returns as a starting point. Say, for example, that you are confident of getting a 10% return per year, you would naturally want to pay us an amount that would make you *more* than 10% per year for our $1000. If you think an additional return of 2% per year is good enough for you, then you could work backwards and discount the $1000 at 12% per year to arrive at a figure that you are willing to pay. For any future cash flow, its present value is given by the formula below:

$$V_0 = \frac{CF_n}{(1+r)^n}$$

V_0 = Present Value
CF_n = Future Cash Flow at year n
r = Discount Rate

If we apply the formula to the current situation, where CF_n = $1000 and $n = 10$, we would get V_0 = $567. This would mean that if you paid us $322 today for $1000 in 10 years' time, you would be getting a 12% compounded return per year — better than the

10% return you would get on your next best idea. So, in short, the "Present Value of Future Cash Flow" can be said to be the opportunity cost of investing in *this* investment instead of the *other* investment and that's the end of our "expound-sation" on the topic. Moving on to the Discounted Cash Flow Model....

We know that we have estimated XYZ Corporation to grow its Free Cash Flow at a terminal rate of 3%. It doesn't really make sense to calculate CF_{5000} and then discount it back to the present. Fortunately, mathematics have provided us with a simple equation that we can use to calculate the present value of all the estimated future free cash flows during the terminal growth phase of the company. It is given as follows:

$$V_{0T} = \frac{CF_n * (1+g_t)}{(r-g_t)(1+r)^n}$$

V_{0T} = Present Value of Free Cash Flow from the business's terminal growth phase

CF_n = Future Cash Flow at year n. In the case of calculating cash flow from the terminal growth phase, year n would be the year just before terminal growth starts. For example, if terminal growth would start at year 11, then n would be equal to 10

r = Discount Rate

g_t = Terminal growth rate

We already have the formula needed to calculate the present value of future cash flows for XYZ Corporation in its higher-growth phases as well as the formula needed for its terminal growth phase. In case you have forgotten, the formula needed to calculate future Cash Flow is given as follows:

$$CF_n = CF_{n-1}\,(1 + g_r)$$

CF_n = Cash Flow at year n

CF_{n-1} = Cash Flow at year $n-1$

g_r = Growth rate

Let's put all these figures, formulas and firecrackers together in one neat package.

Growth Phase	Discount Rate (%)	Formula Needed to calculate Present Value
20% (1st high growth phase)	15	$V_0 = \frac{CF_n}{(1+r)^n}$
10% (2nd high growth phase)	15	$V_0 = \frac{CF_n}{(1+r)^n}$
3% (Terminal growth phase)	15	$V_{0T} = \frac{CF_n * (1+g_t)}{(r-g_t)(1+r)^n}$

The following table shows us how all the calculated figures would look like, starting from the latest Free Cash Flow figure of $2,404,000 found in XYZ Corporation's latest Cash Flow Statement.

Years into the Future	Growth Rate (%)	Undiscounted Free Cash Flow	Discount Rate (%)	Discounted Free Cash Flow	Discount Rate (%)	Discounted Free Cash Flow
0	N.A.	2404000	N.A.	2404000	N.A.	2404000
1	20	2884800	15	2508522	10	2622545
2	20	3461760	15	2617588	10	2860959
3	20	4154112	15	2731396	10	3121046
4	20	4984934	15	2850152	10	3404777
5	20	5981921	15	2974072	10	3714302
6	10	6580113	15	2844765	10	3714302
7	10	7238125	15	2721079	10	3714302
8	10	7961937	15	2602771	10	3714302
9	10	8758131	15	2489607	10	3714302
10	10	9633944	1	2381364	10	3714302
11 till Inifinity	3	N.A.	15	20440038	10	54653308

(5) **Add up all the Free Cash Flow that the business is estimated to be able to generate and divide it by the number of outstanding diluted shares to arrive at Intrinsic Value**

The final step here is simple — we add up all the Discounted Future Free Cash Flows (starting from Year 1) and then divide it by the latest Average No. of Diluted Shares Outstanding to arrive at an estimate of Intrinsic Value using the DCF Model. We shall use the Cash Flow figures derived from the 15% Discount Rate.

The math is presented as follows:

Sum of Future Free Cash Flows = $2,508,522 + $2,617,588.....
+ $20440038 = **$47,161,354**

Intrinsic Value = Sum of Future Free Cash Flows/Average No. of Diluted Shares Oustanding
= $47,161,354 / 10,000,000
= **$4.72**

A summary of the five steps involved in coming up with an Intrinsic Value estimate using the Discounted Cash Flow method is given in the following:

(1) **Calculate the historical CAGR of Free Cash Flow for the business over the last five years.**
(2) **Estimate the future growth rates of Free Cash Flow. Use the historical CAGR of Free Cash Flow together with the qualitative aspects of the business to come up with an estimate for the high-growth rate.**
(3) **Choose a suitable Discount Rate which will be used to discount all the Future Cash Flows back into the present. Calculate the Discounted Future Cash Flows using the Formula given earlier**
(4) **Use the estimated growth rates for Free Cash Flow and the Discount Rate for use in the Discounted Cash Flow model.**

(5) **Add up all the Discounted Free Cash Flow that the business is estimated to be able to generate and divide it by the number of outstanding diluted shares to arrive at Intrinsic Value.**

What Is Wrong with Valuation Models?

We can see that the intrinsic value of $4.72 calculated using the Discounted Cash Flow model is very much smaller than the intrinsic value of $8.35 to $13.92. How can we reconcile this? The easiest way out would be to accept that our estimate of intrinsic value is actually $4.72–$13.92. That is a huge range, and would practically make our estimations worthless. But here in, lies the problem with valuation — it really *is* an art, much more so than a science. Who is to say that our estimation of growth in earnings is too optimistic? Who is to say that our estimation of growth in Free Cash Flow is too small?

So, when faced with situations like this, it will be best to take the more prudent choice and then, keep notes of how fast the intrinsic value of your investments is growing each year to see what kinds of valuation methods are you better in. For example, XYZ Corporation might have grown its Free Cash Flow by 35% for two years into the future, instead of the 20% per year growth we estimated — that would change our estimates of Intrinsic Value and prompt us to better understand where our understanding of the business can be improved.

Measuring the intrinsic value of a business can be precise (we can add 10 decimal places to the Intrinsic Value figure if it makes anyone happier) but it is not necessarily *accurate*. A precise model can have the Intrinsic Value of a business be at $5.923 per share, when in actual fact, it is a lot closer to $10. Perhaps, the best way to describe our thoughts on Intrinsic Value comes from the phrase, *You do not need to know the weight of an obese man to know he is overweight.* When Value presents itself, it usually is fairly obvious.

And, at this point, we hope you would close the book and start to ponder, *Is there something wrong with this valuation method?*

Think — how did we actually estimate the potential growth rate in Step 3 of the Relative Valuation Model? Was it really an informed estimate or was it just a linear projection based on past earnings trends — did we see a pattern and naturally assumed that the pattern will continue?

What will happen if Net Income actually fell in the years that we have projected an increase? We also tend to assume linear growth in companies when in all actuality, businesses do not grow linearly. There are certain years that see massive growth, some years with lacklustre growth and even some years with revenue declines — these are all just facts of life. These are all pitfalls that valuation models present to us, as investors.

Sometimes, we get too anchored to the Intrinsic Value estimates that our model spits out without thinking about changes in the economic or business landscape that might have permanently weakened the earnings power of the business (Anchoring is a concept that we will also explore in later sections under The Mind). This is also a danger that Valuation Models might pose to our investing activities.

Valuation Models also depend inherently on *imprecise and probable* forecasts for the future. In the Relative Valuation Model, we depended upon an estimate of the growth in Net Income; in the Discounted Cash Flow Valuation Model, we depended upon an estimate of the growth in Free Cash Flow. Now, remember we said that humans as a whole are pretty bad at forecasting. So, why do we even bother to forecast if we know it might be a fool's errand? The answer lies in the predictability of a business. There's a slight difference in nuances between "predictability" and "trying to forecast".

What do we mean by this? It means that it is not hard to imagine Coca-Cola selling more soft drinks each year — that's predictability. But, if we were to say Coca-Cola will sell 22.69 million more cans next year compared to last year — that's trying to forecasting. Frankly, no one knows how many exact cans of drinks Coke will sell next year, not even Coke's CEO. So, what we do is, we slap on a growth figure that we think makes sense, and *do not sweat the details.* We watch the businesses grow naturally and will be satisfied if its actual growth is somewhat close to our estimated growth rates. If we predict 20% per year growth for five years, that would mean a cumulative 150% increase and if the business can deliver cumulative growth of 120%, we'll still be happy investors without really being too bothered on what happens each year.

Another great way to overcome the problems of forecasts would be to perform a reverse-engineered Valuation Model.[1] We would take the current share price and calculate what the *implied* growth rate is. For example, let's take XYZ Corporation's current share price to be $3 and run a reverse DCF on it. To do a reverse DCF, we need three things:

1. A Discount Rate
2. The most current FCF figure
3. Current Share Price

We know that XYZ Corporation's most recent FCF figure was $2.404 million. So, we would now tinker with the growth rates until I can get a share price of $3. For simplicity's sake, I would do away with a laddered approach to the growth rates, and will just choose a fixed growth rate (which is the one we will tinker with) for 10 years and then a terminal growth rate of 3%. For the Discount Rate, we'll stick to our previous figure of 15%. We'll keep plugging away Growth Rate figures into our DCF model until we find a growth rate that can give us intrinsic value of $3 per share.

Turns out, a Growth Rate of 9% will yield us an intrinsic value of $3. This means that the market is pricing XYZ Corporation's shares for 9% growth for 10 years, followed by 3% growth to perpetuity. Does a growth figure of 9% make sense to you? Is 9% too high a growth figure or too low a growth figure for you, after doing a Story-study of XYZ Corporation? If you think the growth figure is too low, then that could mean that XYZ Corporation's undervalued to you. If the growth figure is

[1] *Value Investing: Tools and Techniques for Intelligent Investment* by James Montier.

too high, then it could mean that the company's shares are over-valued by the market. The Reverse-DCF helps to take away forecasting error by letting you, the investor, see what kind of growth rates are implied by the market, and then use the Outside Case (the Outside Case will be discussed under The Mind shortly, please be patient with us) to make a suitable judgement.

In conclusion, Valuation Models *must* be used in tandem with an understanding of a business and a good dollop of common sense (the latter is so important, we cannot overstate its importance). And since Valuation Models are so fraught with dangers, we probably should create some buffer for it, don't you think? And that, incidentally, brings us to a concept called Margin of Safety.

Important Questions to ponder about...

1. How important is valuation as part of your investment process?
2. Would you buy a business which you do not understand but appears cheap based on valuation?
3. Does it make sense to use the same valuation method for different types of businesses? For instance, does it make sense to use DCF method on a business with erratic cashflows?

Margin of Safety

> *Confronted with a like challenge to distil the secret of sound investment into three words, we venture the motto, MARGIN OF SAFETY* — Benjamin Graham

Margin of Safety is a very important concept in investing. The phrase itself might deliver its intended meaning to you intuitively. It means that, in investing, even after careful analysis of the Story and the Numbers, we will still insist upon a price that is lower than our estimate of Intrinsic Value. How much lower? That depends on how confident you are in the business.

The concept of Margin of Safety can be traced back to the father of value investing, Benjamin Graham. Back in the 1930s to 1950s, when Graham ran his own hedge fund, the Graham–Newman Partnership, there were many stocks that were being sold very cheaply. Graham used an approach known as Net-Net, which can be loosely translated into an equation as follows:

$$\text{Net-net} = \text{Cash \& Equivalents} + (0.75 \times \text{Accounts Receivable}) + (0.5 \times \text{Inventory}) - \text{Total Liabilities}$$

Graham's aim was to find companies whose market value is 2/3 of their Net-net value. If you are alert, you might notice that a company that is selling below its Net-Net is actually worth more dead than alive. But even so, Graham still insisted upon a Margin of Safety by insisting upon his "2/3" criteria. That is because he knew that errors might creep into his valuation work unknowingly and to prevent himself from paying a dear price for a stock, he set up a Margin of Safety (in Graham's case, the margin would be 33%).

In summary, the whole aim of a Margin of Safety, is literally to leave some room for any unforced errors to come into play and to protect our investment capital as much as possible. To put the Margin of Safety concept into play, we can hack 10%, 20%, 30%, or even 50% off our estimate of Intrinsic Value. In our Relative Valuation calculation for the Intrinsic Value of XYZ Corporation, we came up with an estimate of $8.35 to $13.92. If we put a 20% Margin of Safety into place, we would only buy shares in XYZ Corporation if its price dropped to $6.68 or below.

The key take-away here is to never forget to inject a level of conservatism into our investment activities, and the best way to do so, would be to have a Margin of Safety.

The Mind

The investor's chief problem — and even his worst enemy — is likely to be himself — Benjamin Graham

So here we are, with the last pillar, The Mind, of our tripartite that constitutes a Prudent Investor. Prudent Investing involves the study of a business's management, economic moat, possible future as well as its financial statements to come up with an estimate of intrinsic value that encompasses a margin of safety. However, it takes more than just skills in qualitative and quantitative evaluation of a business to succeed in investing. The control of our emotions is also of utmost importance. As an investor, there are certain mind-sets and emotional qualities that can help us to achieve good investing results. These include patience, contrarianism and scepticism.

Why do we need patience? We need it because *time is the friend of the wonderful business.* A famous General of Ancient Greece, Pericles, once mentioned that we should *wait for the wisest of counsellors — Time.* It is a deeply philosophical phrase but has practical implications for investing as well. Over time, a wonderful business gets recognised by the market and its share price will appreciate along with the increase in its Intrinsic Value. No investor should expect the market to immediately recognise the value of their investments the next day after purchase. Like Charlie Munger says, *Investing is where you find a few great companies and then sit on your ass*, and sitting on your ass essentially means patience!

Contrarianism is the act of doing what others are not — or to simply not be following the herd. However, there is a fine line between being contrarian for the sake of doing it and being contrarian because your logic and study of the facts says that what most people are doing does not make sense. In investing, what usually happens is the general investing public often moves with herd-like behaviour (more on herd-like behaviour shortly). Stock prices can be pushed up to unsustainably high prices when there is euphoria in the market — when everyone else is buying stocks *because everyone else is buying.*

For a little stock market history in the USA, in November 1999, the S&P500 stock market index in the USA was trading at a trailing PE ratio of 26.5 even though its historical and estimated growth rate in earnings was only 6–8% per year.[2] If the S&P500 were a company, its stock price would certainly be way too expensive in relation to its fundamentals. So what could explain the unsustainably high price at which the S&P500 index was trading at? The herd-mentality was largely at work there as more and more speculators bought stocks and pushed prices higher-and-higher because they see everyone else buying and think that it is a reaffirmation that 'investing' in the stock market cannot go wrong. 1999 was part of the infamous Dot-com Bubble and the bubble started to burst from 2000–2002. 'Investors' who followed the crowd got burnt badly as the American Broad Stock Market Index, the S&P 500, fell by more than 50% from its peak in March 2000 (many of these Internet businesses went bust, dragging shareholders' money into oblivion with them).

If an investor at that time had a Contrarian mind-set, he/she might have realised that the stock market as a whole, was at unsustainably high levels and would either opt to stay on the side-lines or make an even gutsier decision and short-sell (when you short-sell a stock, you will make a profit if the stock price falls) the ludicrously priced stocks. Sir John Templeton, famous for his contrarian views in investing, sold-short many Internet-related stocks[3] during the Dot-com bubble and made healthy profits doing so. After all, it was Sir John who wrote, *It is impossible to produce superior performance unless you do something different from the majority* — Now, that's contrarian! But do take note, being a contrarian is not as easy as it seems. It really *hurts* being a contrarian and we will show you in the coming pages.

Scepticism as defined in the dictionary is 'a person inclined to question or doubt accepted opinions' which is similar to contrarianism. However, to be contrarian, you first need to be a sceptic. You need to

---

[2] *Value Investing: From Graham to Buffett and Beyond* by Professor Bruce Greenwald.

[3] *Investing The Templeton Way: The Market-Beating Strategies of Value Investing's Legendary Bargain-Hunter*, by Lauren C. Templeton and Scott Phillips.

be sceptical about the accepted wisdom of the crowds. For example, in 1999 during the Dot-com bubble, when the "professionals" were saying that it is ok that these Internet companies were not making any money and that a more useful way to value these companies would be on "eyeball metrics", i.e., how many people browsed their websites, and throwing away the traditional emphasis on earnings and cash flow out the window. A sceptic will ask, *Is this lack of profitability really okay in the long run?* To quote Warren Buffett, *People get into trouble when they forget that in the long run, stocks won't appreciate faster than the growth in corporate profits.* During the Dot-com bubble, the sceptic would have come to the conclusion that earnings and cash flow do matter in the long run, and any business that cannot operate profitably would eventually have to fold — with shareholders looking back at a big fat ZERO in their investing account!

So, scepticism helps protect you, as an investor, during times of irrational excitement about the stock market. However, with a sceptical mind-set, an investor would also start to question all the doom-and-gloom reports about how the economy will be faring in the long-term future during times of severe recessions or stock-market collapses. As Howard Marks, founder of Oaktree Capital, says, *Scepticism calls for pessimism when optimism is excessive. But it also calls for optimism when pessimism is excessive.* When things look the bleakest, an upturn might just be around the corner.

During the Global Financial Crisis of 2007/2009, financial institutions, hedge funds and individual investors were fleeing the stock market in droves as the S&P500 index fell by almost 57% from peak-to-trough. There were plenty of media commentaries signalling the doom of the economy and stock market. However, at that point in time, the ever-sceptical Warren Buffett wrote an op-ed for *The New York Times* titled *Buy American. I am.* In it, he had a particularly representative statement about calling for optimism when pessimism is excessive — *To be sure, investors are right to be wary of highly leveraged entities or businesses in weak competitive positions. But fears regarding the long-term prosperity of the nation's many sound companies make no sense. These businesses will indeed suffer earnings hiccups, as they always have. But most major companies will be setting new profit records 5, 10 and 20 years from now.*

Buffett's writing was succinct and to the point. He talked about how the use of debt can be dangerous to companies (we discussed this as well in The Numbers) as well as how he was optimistic that the long-term earnings and cash-flow generation powers of strong businesses with durable competitive advantages remained intact. This is how scepticism can help you as an investor during times of crises — by helping you look past the pessimism in the short-term. The S&P500 eventually rebounded by 66% within 1 year from its bottom and has now gone on to within touching distance of its previous 2007 peak at the time of writing. One of Buffett's investments during the height of the 2007/2009 Global Financial Crisis was a US$5 billion investment in Goldman Sachs which earned Buffett US$1.5 billion in dividend payments. After factoring in the total repayment of Goldman Sachs to Buffett for his investment as well as other investment instruments he made in Goldman Sachs (including the dividend payments), Buffett stands to make more than US$3 billion on his US$5 billion investment (or a 60% return in slightly less than four years) at the US bank's share price of $148 (as of the date of writing).

You have now seen how patience, contrarianism and scepticism can help us as investors. However, just knowing these will not guarantee success — our brain has a weird way of harming our investing results because of the way it is works. Most people are prone to making emotional judgements in place of logical ones and in investing, emotion's often the cause of trouble. This brings us to a particularly important yet relatively less well-known aspect of investing — Behavioural Finance.

Behavioural Finance

In most academic finance and economics literature, man has been described as a rational creature with the ability to calculate odds and probabilities precisely and then apply these odds *without emotion* to the activities he is engaged in. There is a fancy term for such a description of mankind — *homo economicus*. However, work done by academics as well as investment professionals in the realm of Behavioural Finance shows that we are actually prone to committing *predictable* cognitive errors that harms our financial health — or *homo mistakus*[1] — and steps can actually be taken to minimise the harmful effects of these cognitive errors. These predictable cognitive errors also stem from our emotions overriding our logic — Benjamin Graham knew about the dangers our emotions can pose to our investment activities long before behavioural finance became a known-word, which explains the nice quote found at the top of this page.

Suppose you have now come up with an expertly calculated intrinsic value (we knew you would absorb the material in The Story and The Numbers well!) of a great business you would like to own. The stock market is roaring and you say, "Well, I'll buy it when the price falls below my intrinsic value". All of a sudden (and it always happens suddenly), the stock market takes a turn for the worse and the business you have been eye-balling for a while suddenly falls way below your

---

[1] *The Little Book of BEHAVIORAL INVESTING: How Not to Be Your Own Worst Enemy* by James Montier.

estimate of intrinsic value as the stock market falls to incredible new lows. Now, would you be buying stocks with glee? As you're reading *Invest Lah!*, you might think 'Of course I'm buying!' Well, chances are, you would not.

Why do we say so? It is because, as humans, we are subjected to an Empathy Gap (a concept which shall be explored in more details later) where there is a difference between what we *think* we will do and what we actually do when we are in a different mental state. This is only one example of how our minds can play tricks on us and harm our investing results. So, let us now embark on a journey inside our head as we look at how we can overcome our worst investing enemy — *ourselves.*

System 1 and System 2 Thinking

Cognitive psychologists have discovered that our mind can be separated into two systems: System 1 and System 2.[2] System 1 thinking is an automatic, fast, instinctive and emotional way of thinking while System 2 is slower, logical and more deliberative. Imagine yourself facing a poisonous snake in a thick glass cage — if the snake rears its head and tries to strike you as move close to it, System 1 would have caused you to recoil from the snake before System 2 can process the fact that there is a solid unbreachable barrier between you and the snake which will keep you completely safe.[3] That is the difference between System 1 and System 2.

System 1 thinking was very important for our early ancestors who were living in the wilderness. Any small, sudden movement in the bushes would have triggered their "fight or flight" response and made them run for their lives in case the movement was due to a large predator. There was no room for error in circumstances like that for

---

[2] *Thinking, fast and slow* by Daniel Kahneman.

[3] *The Little Book of Behavioral Investing: How Not to Be Your Own Worst Enemy* by James Montier.

slow, deliberative thinking as that few additional seconds of thinking might mean the difference between life and death. That is why our body would instinctively jerk away from the snake even though a split second later, our senses would have told us that there was no way the snake could have harmed us.

We would all like to think of ourselves as deliberative, rational human beings where System 2 is used way more often than System 1. However, the truth of the matter is, the influence that System 1 has on our actions is greater than we would like to admit (you must be thinking How can I be affected by my emotions to such a large extent? It must be the others who are doing so. Well.. You have just displayed a common behavioural bias called the Overconfidence Bias. We shall get to that later).

Information is actually processed by System 1 first before System 2 comes into play. System 1 offers a much faster response because it uses short cuts such as the familiarity, similarity and recency of events to make snap judgements[4] — a useful way to describe System 1 thinking would be "quick and dirty". Because of the quick, satisfying nature of System 1 thinking, a lot more information is processed by it and thus a majority of our actions are actually controlled by System 1 thinking as System 2 slumbers lazily in the background. Or as Daniel Kahneman, one of the foremost authorities on Behavioural Economics (closely linked to Behavioural Finance) puts it, *We run mostly on System 1 software.*[5]

This very brief primer on how our mind operates would be useful in our discussion of some of the common behavioural quirks that affects most of us and can lead to poor investment results. Evolution occurs at a glacial pace and the parts of our brain responsible for System 1 thinking has remained with us even in modern times. Actually, System 1 thinking is also important in modern life — think of how

---

[4] *The Little Book of Behavioral Investing: How Not to Be Your Own Worst Enemy* by James Montier.

[5] *Your Money and Your Brain* by Jason Zweig.

you swerved to avoid danger in traffic when you spot any danger — but it can be hazardous to your wealth.

Calling System 1 and System 2 — Are you ready?

Loss Aversion

Simply put, Loss Aversion is the tendency for us to feel more "psychological pain" as compared to a "psychological gain" when losing or gaining by an equivalent amount respectively in any sort of activity. Imagine that you are playing a game[6] where you are given two options: (1) A sure chance of winning \$1000 and (2) 80% chance of winning \$1500 and 20% chance of winning nothing. What's your option? We're pretty sure you've picked Option 1 (relax, we can't read your mind, but we sure can pick out behavioural biases!).

Now, imagine another game where you are again given two options: (1) Lose \$1000 for sure or (2) 80% of losing \$1500 and 20% chance of losing nothing. Take your pick — we won't peek. However, we're again pretty sure that you've picked Option 2. If you had taken a bit of time to do the math, you might have come up with the table shown below:

	Game 1	Game 2
Expected Outcome for Option 1	\$1000	-\$1000
Expected Outcome for Option 2	\$1200	-\$1200

The *Expected Outcome* for Option 1 of both games is pretty straightforward. For Option 2, the *Expected Outcome* calculation requires a little work. For Option 2, Game 1, the *Expected Outcome* is given as: *Expected Outcome* = (\$1500 × 0.80) + (\$0 × 0.20) = \$1200. Similarly, for Option 2, Game 2, the *Expected Outcome* is given as: *Expected Outcome* = (−\$1500 × 0.80) + (\$0 × 0.20) = −\$1200.

So, from the table, you could see that it would have been the *logical* choice to pick Option 2 in Game 1 and Option 1 in Game 2. However,

[6] *Ibid.*

most people would have picked the opposite choices instead, because the *sure losses are painful to System 1.* The emotional part of our thinking takes over and makes us pick the less logical choice.

How can this titbit of information help us in investing, you might ask. Have you had friends or family who have bought losing stocks only to say *We'll sell when it goes up* even though the stock represents ownership in a company that is so obviously broken that chances of recovery are minuscule? Part of their refusal to make a logical decision to sell is because of Loss Aversion — the act of selling turns a paper loss into reality and it is painful for our brains to process this loss even though the logical choice would have been to take those losses and deploy the remaining capital into other much better opportunities elsewhere.

Availability Bias

The Availability Bias refers to the tendency for people to *assess the relative importance of issues by the ease with which they are retrieved from memory.*[7] A great example of the Availability Bias at work happened in the aftermath of the tragic September 11, 2001 case when terrorist forces crashed two planes into the World Trade Centre in New York City and another plane into part of the Pentagon. After the terrorist attacks, fear of terrorist hijacking planes became the talk of the town in USA and the general public were reminded of the incident frequently across all forms of media. Because of that, more Americans took to the roads rather than taking a plane, but the real danger was that in USA, a person is 65 times more likely to die while driving than taking a plane.[8] The Availability Bias has clouded people's judgement when assessing the real risks of car travel as opposed to air travel and this same Availability Bias can also cloud your judgement on the real risks of investing.

In a roaring bull-market, when stock prices go in only one direction — up! — you are constantly reminded of how well the stock

[7] *Thinking, Fast and Slow* by Daniel Kahneman.

[8] *Your Money and Your Brain* by Jason Zweig.

market is doing in daily news media; of how stock XYZ has gone up 100% in its first day since its IPO; and of how your next-door neighbour and favourite nasi-lemak hawker has made a bundle in the stock market based on tips. Thus, the most *easily accessible* memory you will have of the stock market is that of ever-rising stock prices. This is dangerous because stock-prices do not keep rising without reason. It has to be backed up by a business's earnings and cash flow. However, in stock market bubbles, like the 1999 Dot-Com bubble, stock prices rose to irrationally high levels that were not backed by any possible increases in earnings of the underlying businesses. When the Availability Bias makes you associate stocks with ever-rising prices without regard to the underlying growth in profits, it can harm your investing results.

Likewise, during times of major stock market declines or economic recessions, stories of investors who have lost their personal fortunes in the stock market, countries in financial difficulties, corporations going bankrupt and more are constantly in the news. This puts negative associations with stock-market investing into the forefront and thus makes it an *easily accessible* memory. You are now more likely than ever to associate stock market investing with risky behaviour and losing money without considering the base case that the markets moves in cycles and that it is the best time to buy when the situation looks the most dire. Our emotional-thinking, the product of System 1, has negative connotations regarding the stock market as its most easily accessible memory and might cloud our judgement. After all, Sir John Templeton once said *The time of maximum pessimism is the best time to buy and the time of maximum optimism is the best time to sell.* Even though the Availability Bias makes it seem that bad situations will go on indefinitely, but the fact of the matter is, things do and have always recovered.

Empathy Gap

The Empathy Gap, which was briefly mentioned earlier, is the tendency for us to exhibit a difference between what we *think* we would do and what we *actually do* when we are in a different mental state. Duke

University's Professor of Psychology and Behavioural Economics, Dan Ariely, conducted an experiment[9] involving male college students that rammed home the impact of the Empathy Gap. The experiment consisted of questions related to sexual behaviour and the possible answers to each question contained a range from "no" to "yes". So, each participant was made to answer the questions and the answers were tallied. A few days later, they were given the same set of questions, but with a different set of instructions — they were asked to answer the questions while masturbating to an erotic film. The answers were again collated and something surprising emerged.

The first time the questions were answered corresponded to a "cold" mental state while in the second attempt, the male college students were considered to be in an "aroused" mental state. The results showed that the exact same participants' desire to engage in odd sexual behaviour increased by almost twice in the "aroused" mental state as compared to the "cold" mental state. This *is* the empathy gap in action! The participants clearly could not anticipate how much they might change in their "aroused" mental state.

When this idea is translated into the investing arena, it becomes a simple case of us being paralyzed by fear and being unable to buy during bear markets or being overwhelmed by ever increasing stock prices and being unwilling to sell during a bull market for fear of 'missed' gains. When the markets are going sideways or going up, it is easy to say *I will be a buyer of stocks when the stock market starts to go down* but in reality, because of the empathy gap, the process is not as easy as we think. A similar thing can happen before a sustained bull-market rally in which we have stocks we would like to sell at particular prices that makes sense when compared to the business fundamentals but because of how much stock prices have increased, we are blinded by Greed (discussed later) and now become unable to sell our stocks even though the stock prices might have risen to levels that cannot be supported by any fundamental signs.

---

[9] *Predictably Irrational* by Dan Ariely.

Outcome Bias

Imagine yourself in a casino and being dealt an 8 and a Queen in a game of Black Jack. For some reason, you felt extremely lucky and asked to be dealt another card. It turns out to be a 3 and you make 21 points, beating the dealer's hand in the process while everyone around congratulates you for having the guts to make a great play. Sounds good does it? However, if you think for a moment on the odds behind your chances of coming away with a positive outcome on that hand, it might not seem such a great move after all.

In Black Jack, the objective of the game is to get as close to 21 points as possible — exceed 21 points, and you lose the game. So, for a hand that contains an 8 and a Queen (a Queen is equivalent to 10 points in Black Jack), only four more points would make that hand go bust. There are 52 cards in a poker deck, and the only cards that would give a positive outcome would be an Ace (which can count as 1 point), a 2 and a 3. There are four suits for each particular card and so, your chances of picking an advantageous card would be only 12/52, or only 23%. If the casino can get away with similar odds of 77% for winning each hand on all their games, they would go out of business *really* soon — no sane gambler would want to gamble there!

In short, that imagined Black Jack game was used to illustrate a good outcome but *bad process*. The sad thing about our brains is that, we tend to focus on the *outcomes* and not the process (yes, I'm looking at YOU, System 1). A scientific study[10] involved participants' evaluation of a surgeon's decision to send his patient for surgery. The scenarios described in the study are briefly shown as follows:

1. A patient is in his mid-50s and has a heart condition that causes pain and interferes with his work and life. A surgeon suggests that the patient go ahead with a heart by-pass surgery that would eradicate the pain and increase his life expectancy from 65 to 70.

[10] *The Little Book of Behavioral Investing: How Not to Be Your Own Worst Enemy* by James Montier.

However, 8% of such operations results in death. The operation was eventually found to be successful.

2. Exactly the same as above, except that the operation was not successful.

Logically speaking, the quality of the surgeon's decision should not be predicated on the outcome of the surgery because the surgeon could not have known the outcome of the surgery *before* he performed it. However, participants in the study would rate Scenario 1 much more highly than Scenario 2 — because they had allowed the emotional outcome of the decision to influence their rating process.

In investing, there are times we might be lucky and hit upon the jackpot by buying into penny-stocks with no Earnings and minimal Assets or entered a short-term trade thinking we knew exactly how the price of the stock would react in the short-term. However, this is not a repeatable process and if we mistake a good outcome with a good process and blindly chase after investment returns built upon speculative behaviour and a bad process, the *eventual* outcome will more often than not turn out to be disastrous.

Overconfidence Bias

We're going to assume you hold a driver's license and play a real quick game with you. Do you think you are a better than average driver? Note down your answer and ask all your friends who hold driving licenses the same question (Do not worry, we will be waiting). Did everybody else's answer surprise you? Most people would actually answer "yes", so much so that roughly 75% of drivers turn out to be better than average drivers — notice the intense irony in that statement[11]? What this shows is a classic behavioural bias that afflicts almost all of us — the Overconfidence Bias.

[11] *Your Money and Your Brain* by Jason Zweig.

Studies have been conducted on people of diverse professions on the perils of Overconfidence.[12] For example, a study was done on stock market analysts who were asked to give the probability that a stock would exceed a certain price by a given date. It was found that on average, the stock market analysts were 80% confident but only 60% accurate. Yet another example involved 3,000 entrepreneurs who had recently launched their own business.[13] The entrepreneurs were asked a series of questions:

1. What are the chances of success for a business like yours?
2. What are the chances of your business succeeding?

For Question 1, only 39% of the participants felt that a business similar to theirs had a greater than 7/10 chance of success. However, when answering Question 2, 81% of the participants felt their *own* business had a greater than 7/10 chance of success! This is akin to *everyone* saying they are better than average. How can that be? Statistics have shown instead that roughly 50% of new businesses fail within their first five years.

What has it got to do with investing you might ask? Well, Overconfidence can manifest itself in us thinking that we *know a lot* about an investment and thus can predict its share price movements with high confidence. This can lead us to jump in and out of our stocks, thinking that we know what the flavour of the month or (horror of horrors!) flavour of the week is. Overconfidence might also affect us in a subtle way when we think we know a business well enough to invest in when in actual fact, we might not even know exactly how the business earns its money!

Anchoring

Anchoring is this curious effect where we grasp at a totally irrelevant number as the basis for making any decision that involves numbers.

[12] *Contrarian Investment Strategies: The Psychological Edge* by David Dreman.
[13] *Your Money and Your Brain* by Jason Zweig.

For example, if we were to ask you to write down the last four digits of your mobile phone number and then asked you to guess the distance between Earth and the dwarf planet Pluto, your guess of the distance would be affected by your mobile phone number — even though there is no logical link whatsoever.

To see the effect clearly, try the same test on friends who have the last four digits of their mobile phone number above 7,000 and less than 3,000. For the friends who have the last four digits of their mobile phone numbers above 7,000, collect their answers in one group and find the average. Do the same for friends who have the last four digits of their mobile phone numbers less than 3,000. We are willing to bet that there will be a marked difference in the average of their guesses for the distance between Earth and Pluto — the ones who have the last four digits of their mobile numbers above 7,000 will have higher guesses than the other group. This is the Anchoring effect in action — a totally irrelevant number (mobile phone numbers) has had an effect on the estimate of another number or decision (the distance between Earth and Pluto).

In Jason Zweig's *Your Money and Your Brain*, he wrote about how behavioural psychologists Amos Tversky and Daniel Kahneman asked people to spin a wheel of fortune that was numbered from 0 to 100. After spinning the wheel, the participants were asked to estimate whether the percentage of United Nations membership made up by African countries was higher or lower than the number they had just spun. It should be no surprise to you now to know that spinning the wheel of fortune affected the participants' estimates, even though the wheel of fortune number is totally random and irrelevant — on average, people who spun a 10 guessed that 25% of United Nations members were African countries while people who spun a 65 guessed the percentage to be 45%.

In investing, Anchoring effects can appear when we might have subconsciously used a company's current stock price as a starting point to adjust our estimate of Intrinsic Value[14] — remember how we mentioned that it is very easy to come up with an Intrinsic Value that satisfies us, instead of a figure that conforms to the economic realities of the business.

Anchoring effects might also appear when we have calculated the Intrinsic Value of the business *before* checking its stock price but then fail to lower (increase) our Intrinsic Value estimates adequately due to a permanent impairment (improvement) of a business's earnings power as the economic and business landscape changes. The overly high (low) initial estimate of Intrinsic Value makes it hard to adjust the Intrinsic Value estimate downwards (upwards), in effect 'pulling' the subsequent adjustments towards the initial estimate.

Greed

Greed should be a very familiar concept for all of us. Whenever we head to our favourite buffet restaurants — one of our nation's favourite past-times — and see people piling up their plates with food, we often think *Wow, they sure are greedy!* Over-eating on a one-off basis would cause only temporary discomfort, but Greed in the stock market, might just mean *permanent* wealth destruction.

It might come as a surprise to you, but the act of winning a financial bet actually does not stimulate your brain as much as *expecting* the win. When you place a bet in any form of gamble (and remember that investing is actually a calculated gamble), the mere anticipation of a possible win floods our brain with 'feel-good' chemicals. Too much of these, and it can become an addiction. That is why gambling can become an addiction — the mere *thought* of making a quick buck feels so good to our brain that it craves that feeling over and over again.

Greed is particularly dangerous in investing when it comes to the promise of a quick buck in the IPO du jour or in the next hottest growth

[14] *Contrarian Investment Strategies: The Psychological Edge* by David Dreman.

stock. Investing on a tip from "well-informed" sources is incredibly seductive, not so much because of the accuracy and quality of the tip (we certainly think such tips should be avoided as much as possible — *unless*, the tip came from Warren Buffett or Peter Lynch — in which case, please get us in touch with them!), but because of the possibility of a quick buck. Remember, it is the anticipation of a quick buck that feels so good and addictive, and any tip that has the potential to earn you some money quickly will be very attractive to your brain.... but very harmful for your wallet.

Forecasting

For those of you who think it is an absolute necessity to know; what the global economy is going to do; how much long-term interest rates will change; or what industry is going to perform well over the next twelve months before you can safely invest, raise your hands. If not, stop lying (we are joking here, of course)!

It is common to feel that it is important to know what the future might bring when it comes to investing. After all, when we invest, we are making a calculated gamble that the future of the business we are invested in will be better than its present. However, if you invest thinking economic and financial forecasts are vital in investing, you might do better if you throw some darts at a dartboard.

Phillip Tetlock did a study involving 82,000 different forecasts from various experts in domains that include economics, legal opinions, climate, politics and financial markets among many others. He found out that the accuracy of their forecasts was *no better than a coin flip*. David Dreman[15] did a study on analysts' forecasts of companies' earnings results from 1973–2010 and found out that the chance of a stock not having any surprises (i.e., deviating more than 5% from the forecasts) for 10 quarters was 1 in 199,000. Those are astronomically

[15] *Contrarian Investment Strategies: The Psychological Edge* by David Dreman.

high-odds, meaning analysts have *very* little chance of getting things spot on.

One of the reasons why people can be so bad at forecasts is because of the phenomenon of the "Inside View" versus the "Outside View". When using the "Inside View", the forecasters are really concerned with all the attributes that concern the event that he is trying to forecast, paying no attention whatsoever to similar events that have occurred in the past. The "Outside View" is just the opposite. It takes into account what has happened historically to all other similar cases to come up with logical conclusions. Most forecasters focus their energies with the "Inside View" rather than the "Outside View".

A good example of the "Inside View" and "Outside View" phenomenon was recounted by Daniel Kahneman.[16] He joined a team of education experts to come up with a curriculum that includes course materials, textbooks, practise problems, etc. to teach judgement and decision making in high school. After making good progress for a year, they all came up with estimates on how long it would take for them to finish the project. All of them thought they could complete the project within two years as they were confident of their abilities. Kahneman asked another expert within the team who had a lot of experience in similar projects in the past, how long did other groups of similar ability actually take to finish similar projects after making as much progress as the current team had? The answer was stunning — around 40% of such teams failed to complete the projects and even then, those who completed such projects took at least seven years! The experienced expert that Kahneman questioned was surprised at himself that he did not even think about his experience with other teams when estimating a completion time for the current team. He had been using the "Inside View" rather than the "Outside View"!

In investing, we would often use the "Inside View" when looking at companies. We like to think about how the business can grow, what

[16] *Thinking, fast and slow* by Daniel Kahneman.

new markets they can explore and then apply these growth estimates into our estimate of Intrinsic Value. However, the correct thing to do would be to look at the base-case rates of how other firms have evolved. For example, only 0.01% of corporations in the USA have managed to grow at rates of 22% and above for 10 years.[17] If we think the businesses that we partially own can grow at rates of 20% or higher for 10–15 years, then we better have a very, very good reason to think so, because the odds of it happening are *really low*.

Herd Behavior

There's this old refrain saying *There's safety in numbers*. In nature, that is absolutely true. That is why we can see spectacular displays of herding in animals — schools of fish, prides of lions, flocks of birds and so on. Even among humans, we generally like to live in communities because as neighbours, we can help each other in times of need and we feel safe knowing there's friends and family near us. However, in investing, safety certainly does *not* come in numbers.

We (the authors) have been through our teenage years and can attest to the power of peer pressure; how we think a certain bag or shoe looks cool because our peers are carrying it; or how certain slang words are desirable because everyone else is using it. We're sure most of you are familiar with peer pressure as well but studies have been conducted on this phenomenon and show a dangerous tendency for conformation, even to the extent of being "blind" to facts.

Consider a study[18] where people were asked to judge whether some three-dimensional objects were different or the same. Participants sometimes answered the questions in isolation, while at other times, they were shown the answers that four computers or four peers (who were actually colluding with the researchers and picked all the wrong

[17] *The Little Book of Behavioral Investing: How Not to Be Your Own Worst Enemy* by James Montier.

[18] *Your Money and Your Brain* by Jason Zweig.

choices on purpose) had chosen before answering the questions themeselves. Participants who answered in isolation were right 84% of the time while those who were shown answers by four computers got it right only 68% of the time. The interesting point of this study happened when participants who were shown the answers by four peers only got their choices right 59% of the time. When exposed to the choices of their peers, these participants felt a lot more compulsion to follow the choices of their peer group, even if these choices do not correspond to facts.

Brain scans were also done on the participants during the study and it was found that participants who picked the same choices as the four-peer group had showed a decrease in the parts of the brain that handled our System 2 thinking. In other words, when they were following a group, or "Herding", they simply stopped thinking logically.

There have also been experiments conducted to study how social exclusion (which is a practical consequence of going against the herd) can actually cause pain to the excluded individuals. Participants in a particular experiment were made to play a three-way game where a ball is thrown back and forth among the players.[19] The other two players were actually controlled by computers and after a while, those players would ignore the participant by passing the ball only among themselves. Brain activities of the participants were measured during the study and it was found that regions of the brain that are activated by real physical pain were also highly active when the participants were excluded from the ball game. If being a contrarian entails social exclusion (and it often does), then our brain does makes it really hard for anyone to be a true contrarian!

In investing, because of the need to follow the crowd, we would also tend to look for confirmation from others that we are making a good investment and feel pain when the majority disagrees with our investing choices. This is dangerous because the most popular stocks are often bid to unsustainably high prices, setting the stage for a precipitous price decline. In contrast, the most unloved stocks (and often some of

---

[19] *The Little Book of Behavioral Investing: How Not to Be Your Own Worst Enemy* by James Montier.

the best investing opportunities) are at great bargain prices but are the most painful ones to invest in. The sense of fear is heightened during a general market collapse, when everyone else is selling stocks. This makes investing at that time a really hard thing to do because it is the exact opposite of what the majority is doing.

Framing

The last behavioural bias we are going to discuss (and this is by no means an exhaustive list) concerns a curious concept known as Framing.

Psychologists Amos Tversky and Nobel Laureate Daniel Kahneman once ran a now-classic study on the phenomenon of framing that involved 2 groups of college students.[20] The first group was presented with this scenario:

> Imagine the USA preparing for the outbreak of an unusual disease that will kill 600 people. Two programs are proposed as a possible solution for the outbreak, of which their exact estimated statistical outcomes are known:
>
> 1. Program A: If adopted, 200 people will be saved.
> 2. Program B: If adopted, there is a 1/3 probability that 600 people will be saved and a 2/3 probability that no one will be saved.

The second group was presented with this scenario:

> Imagine the USA preparing for the outbreak of an unusual disease that will kill 600 people. Two programs are proposed as a possible solution for the outbreak, of which their exact statistical outcomes are known:
>
> 1. Program C: If adopted, 400 people will die.
> 2. Program B: If adopted, there is a 1/3 probability that nobody will die and a 2/3 probability that 600 people will die.

[20] *Your Money and Your Brain* by Jason Zweig.

Both groups were asked which options they would pick and the results were truly surprising. Around 72% of students in the first group picked Program A, while only 22% of students in the second group picked Program C, even though *both programs were identical!* It was only the wording that was altered, in other words, the exact same information was *Framed* differently. Program A was Framed in a positive way, emphasizing the lives that can be saved and hence appealed more to the student participants. Usually, when information's framed in terms of a sure gain as opposed to a sure loss even though the end result would be the same for both situations, people would pick the sure-gain scenario more often than not. Or, in lay-man speak, people would always pick the exact same information presented in a happy-way over the one presented in a sad-way.

Framing can be hazardous from a personal finance point of view. If given a choice between a 4% or 0% increase in your salary, we would not be getting any prizes for thinking you would pick the first option. Now, let's change the options up a little. Choose between a 4% salary increase at an inflation rate of 3% and a 0% increase in salary with inflation at 2%.[21] The rational choice should have been the latter option, but because of Framing — in which they can see the salary increase but not the inflation that's eating at their purchasing power — most people end up choosing the former option instead.

Weaving It All Together

So, you are now aware of some of the common behavioural biases that might affect our investing results. But, behavioural biases are still *there* even if you are aware of them. The act of awareness itself does not take away the risk, just as driving at 200 km/h on sharp bends does not diminish the risk of a fatal accident even if you are aware of its dangers. What we can do is to have sub-optimal solutions to *lessen* the negative

---

[21] *Your Money and Your Brain* by Jason Zweig.

impact that our emotions can have on our investing activities. Some of these solutions presented here are what we have actually been doing in our own retail investing activities. Some are what we have learnt from books that we will implement in the future.

These solutions also do not have a 1-for-1 correspondence with any particular behavioural biases, but rather, when taken together, they can help to minimise the negative financial impacts of all these biases.

Of course, the list presented below is by no means exhaustive and we would think we have succeeded with one of our aims of writing this book if you actually come up with your own additional way of dealing with emotions — or rather, not letting emotions dictate your investing.

Without further ado, here are some of the ways we can prevent our brains from messing our investments up:

1. **Keep an investing journal and a wish list of stocks you want to purchase**

   The investing journal should contain our thoughts on buying/selling, as well as the feelings running through our mind *before* any buy/sell order's executed. Putting our thoughts and feelings on paper helps to activate System 2 thinking, which brings our logic into play.

   The wish list contains a list of prices of different stocks that you think would make great bargains. More importantly, the list is done up in times when the market's going up or when it is calm. During times of market turmoil, whip this list out and start buying! The idea of being prepared in normal conditions is that our emotions have a lesser effect on us when we are deciding on what to buy. In a financial market or economic collapse, when everything is a sea of red, fear kicks in and we might act irrationally, hence the need to be prepared. Having a wish list helps us to override our emotions and prevents us from being paralysed by our emotions when the best times to buy start appearing on the market.

2. **Focus on Outcomes**

A simple matrix explaining how outcomes and processes interact with each other that first appeared in Russo and Schoemaker's book, *Winning Decisions* is shown below. Basically, we should always strive to have our actions appear in the top left quadrant of the table and avoid the bottom right quadrant (for illustration purposes, the winning Black Jack hand described in **Outcome Bias** would be "Dumb Luck", while the failed surgery described in Scenario 2 of the scientific study would be "Bad Break"). A good process in investing is of *paramount importance* because only with a good process can our chances of eventual success be dramatically increased.

	Good Outcome	**Bad Outcome**
Good Process	Deserved Success	Bad Break
Bad Process	Dumb Luck	Poetic Justice

3. **Have a "Too Hard" Pile**

Charlie Munger was quoted as saying *I have three mail boxes in my mailbox — In, Out and Too Hard.* What Munger is saying is that for businesses he does not understand, he immediately chucks them into the "Too Hard" pile and looks at the ones he can understand. Ser Jing often jokes about how banks and financial institutions go straight into his "Too Hard" pile. The "Too Hard" pile is a very good tool to overcome Overconfidence because if we ask ourselves the question "Do we understand the business and its money-making activities well?", we can answer with Yes, No or Maybe. You already know that we are all prone to being overconfident of our own abilities and if we *think* we only have a mediocre understanding of a business, we probably actually know next to nothing about the business! By eliminating potential investment choices this way, we can save ourselves a lot of grief by having companies with opaque operations blow up on us through careless risk-taking by management or outright fraud.

4. **Set aside a small, very small, sum of money for speculation within your investment portfolio**

We all know the allure of a gamble and how we now know just *why* it is that a speculative gamble feels almost… irresistible. Thus, we suggest that you give in to your Greed. What!? Give in to it!? Why, yes — to give in to Greed is to acknowledge that we can all be somewhat susceptible to its powerful grasp and to satiate the desire for easy money, we can set aside very small portions of our investable portfolio (say 1–2%) for these gambles. If they work out, everyone goes home happy. If it doesn't, we would still have scratched that gambling itch and can rest assured that our investing portfolio is largely unharmed and long-term compounding can continue to work its magic to build our wealth.

5. **Focus on Your Portfolio and Tune Out the Noise**

Nobody would be happy with a stock that loses 50% and we might often panic when such an event occurs. But, if we think in terms of how much the stock represents as part of our portfolio, the total monetary effect of that 50% drop in stock prices might be diminished and make it easier to stomach that temporary decline in share price. For example, if it represents 5–10% of a well-diversified portfolio (diversified over different economic climates, different market cycles, different value points — but that's another story for another day), the overall impact would be only 2.5–5%. It is painful, yes, but nothing that can really make you lose your sleep and mess up your proper investing process. There will also be times when your favourite winner "falls" from a 500% gain to a 300% gain (such is the fate of most high PE stocks, but we're digressing) and you feel unhappy about it. But think again, if this stock was bought 10 years ago and you went to a paradise island with no internet or phone access and came back today to see your stock had risen by 300% for an annual compounded return of 11.6% per year, would you be happy? We certainly would!

You already know how susceptible you might be to following the herd, so tune out all that market chatter from the likes of CNBC and focus instead on what is truly important — can the business that you have purchased a part ownership of earn even more money in the future? Following all the rumours and gossips can only lead to more emotional behaviour because only sensationalized news attracts readers. While it is important to follow important events for your investments, such as the business signing new contracts or selling new products etc., businesses often do not change overnight.

6. **Keep Calm and Carry on**

There is always a constant source of worry. Like Peter Lynch said, *There is always something to worry about. Avoid weekend thinking and ignore the latest dire predictions of the newscasters.* Economic prognosticators and soothsayers will often have various views about where the economy and the financial markets are heading and it can sometimes seem daunting, even scary. But, in investing, we are trying to find bargains — we are trying to buy parts of a business at a price that is much smaller than what it will be worth in the future. Because of that, what we really need to do, is to focus on the business and invest when we think it presents a bargain. It doesn't really matter if interest rates go up or down or if the unemployment rate is going to increase by 2.3452% by 31 February 2030 — people will still want goods and services that they value. So, find a good business to invest in, invest in it and then keep calm and carry on.

Important Questions to ponder about…

1. Have you experienced any of the above mentioned psychological bias in your life?
2. Now that you're aware of such psychological bias, which do you think you are more prone to?
3. Can you think of some ways to turn the bias into your advantage?

Circle of Competence

> *There's a whole bunch of things I don't know a thing about. I just stay away from those. I stay within what I call my circle of competence*
> — Warren Buffett

As Prudent Investors, we know how much our minds can play tricks on us in our investing activities. Because of that, it is very important to know what we know and what we *don't* know. Buffett was well-known for coining the term "Circle of Competence" for describing the kinds of businesses he understands and those that he doesn't. And then, he would insist on staying well within the boundaries of his "Circle". To invest in a business, we first have to understand the business.

We want to invest in businesses that are simple and easy to understand. You know how Starhub makes money and it is a simple business to understand. You know how SPH makes money and it is a simple business to understand. You know how SIA makes money and it is a simple business to understand. We are not saying the above businesses are good businesses to invest in. We still need to look into other parts of the business like the management, financial statements, valuation and possible future catalysts (will be covered later). An easy-to-understand business may not be a good investment but that is a good start. When you understand the business, it is easier to look into it further than one which you do not understand at all. What other businesses do you understand? To answer that easily, think of the following:

- In which industry and company do you work?
- What are your interests?
- What products do you use daily?
- What do you spend money on?
- Where do you shop?
- What do you observe around you when you go shopping?
- What do you observe when you are travelling on the roads or in the trains?

We call this the "Circle of Competence". By looking within the realm of this circle, we are able to research into the businesses that you understand and thus, are more likely to love investing in those wonderful businesses. The businesses will have meaning to you and investing does not become a chore but more of something you enjoy doing. Warren Buffett had this to say about circle of competence — "You don't have to be an expert on every company, or even many. You only have to be able to evaluate companies within your circle of competence. The size of that circle is not very important; knowing its boundaries, however, is vital."

Sometimes, researching into a business will make you feel like a Private Investigator (PI, Prudent Investment — pun intended!) researching into a case. That's what Sudhan feels whenever he researches into a business. He feels he puts on the hat of Sherlock Holmes and this makes investing fun!

Once you have identified the business that you like, you have to look into the business model. The following questions will help you:

- What industry does the business operate in?
- What products or services does the business provide?
- How does it make money from the products and services it provides?
- Are the future earnings predictable?
- Who are its competitors?
- Is the business sustainable? Will the products or services the company provides be obsolete in 5–10 years' time?

Important Questions to ponder about…

1. Is it wise to invest in something you do not understand?
2. What questions can you ask yourself to define your circle of competence?
3. Can you also name some industries and companies which are NOT within your circle of competence?

Consolidation: Putting Everything We Have Learnt Together

What to Do?

In summary, we have just gone through how to look at businesses qualitatively (The Story), quantitatively (The Numbers) and helped you learn a little more about behavioural psychology and how it can affect your investing results (The Mind).

Looking for Stocks

- Your circle of competence
    - In which industry and company do you work?
    - What are your interests?
    - What products do you use daily?
    - What do you spend money on?
    - Where do you shop?
    - What do you observe around you when you go shopping?
    - What do you observe when you are travelling on the roads or in the trains?
- Friends, family, colleagues, investment clubs
- Magazines
- Forums

- Stock screeners
- Basically, everywhere!
- Once you have noticed about a company, next look if they are listed and if they are, investigate into the business further with the framework given in this book

Investigating Stocks and Buying Them

- Use the framework given in the book (list the criteria needed).
- Keep an open mind and do not make a decision until you've performed a thorough analysis.
- When buying, don't be too concerned about buying it $0.005 cheaper. If it's undervalued, you can always buy it at market price.

  Wei Lin prefers to set market orders because he thinks it's better to have paid a tad more for a great business than to miss out on a huge ride because of a small difference in the market price and the price he is willing to pay for the business. However, should you do this for illiquid stocks (low volume), be prepared that you might end up paying more than the last done price.
- Once you buy them, think as if the stock market will be closed for the next 10 years. You do not have to constantly monitor the stock price. Staring at the Teletex or computer screen will not make stock prices move the way you want it to. Only proper execution by your chosen business leaders leading to increased or decreased (touch wood!) profits would move stock prices, *over the long run.*
- Keep track of your purchase details like date bought, buy price, commissions, etc.
- Before investing in a stock, write down reasons for buying it. *And,* reasons that will make you sell.

Monitoring Stocks

- It is a buy-and-monitor and not a buy-and-hold strategy.
- Monitor the business and not the daily stock price!

- If it's a retail or F&B business, visit the stores and see if everything is as per normal.
- Every year, look at the yearly results and see if the business is still intact (the reasons you bought the business for still stands). You do not have to bother about quarterly results as it's too short-term. But, it will be great to take note of what's happening every quarter as well. Perhaps, new stores might be opening or new acquisitions might be coming, these can change estimates of intrinsic value as well.
- Revert back to our checklist on Financial Statement Analysis for some important numbers to monitor every year. Remember, the checklist is by no means the *only* way to do it — you might decide to tweak the list to suit your own investing temperament and style. By all means, please do so!
- Do not get too hung up over Economic forecasts and stock market predictions.
- Go for AGMs and ask questions. Mingle with like-minded investors.

When to Sell

- Sell when the fundamentals have turned for the worse.
- Sell when there are better opportunities.
- Selling when the price is overvalued is a bit iffy. One can choose to hold on to the business even if the price is overvalued, provided the fundamentals are still the same.
- If the business is still growing and valuations have not gone over the roof, then "taking profit" might not necessarily be a good idea.
- Automatic "stop loss" orders, meaning to say an order is set so as to sell the business once the stock price falls by a certain percentage might not be a good idea. If short-term market shocks or one-off negative events cause a big drop in the stock price, it might trigger a sell automatically. When the sale occurs, you incur commissions and then, have to fret on when to buy it back in again. When you do buy, you have to incur commissions yet again. It would be better

on the psyche and on your wallet to just hold on through blips and bumps. For what it's worth, a huge drop in share price might actually be a great opportunity to accumulate more shares in the business.

- Once you sell, calculate your returns.
- Every year, calculate your total portfolio returns using XIRR (simple to do using Excel). Compare your returns with the benchmark index, e.g. STI. If you cannot beat the market over five years, it is better off to invest in the STI ETF. Do not be discouraged even if you can't beat the market. It is not easy to beat the market but it is easy to invest and get market-like returns. If there's a disciplined approach to investing, even in the STI ETF, an investor will very likely achieve inflation-thumping returns, thereby growing the investor's purchasing power.

Company Case Studies

Even after knowing by heart all the squishy topics about management effectiveness, corporate culture and Economic Moats and the hard-numbers topics about Financial Statements and Valuations, it might be hard to piece them all together. But, fear not as we will now show some examples of local companies to bring you through our thought process and how we go about looking at their Story and their Numbers.

Vicom

Overview of Vicom

Vicom is Singapore's leading provider in technical testing and inspection services. Vicom also has a non-vehicular testing and inspection business called Setsco.

The business is recession-proof. Even during a recession, vehicles have to be sent for inspection. Also, government regulations bode well for this business where cars have to be sent for inspection biennially every 3–10 years (more information below).

Table 1.1. Inspection Price and Schedule List for vehicles in Singapore

	Inspection Fees		Inspection Frequency		
Vehicle Category	**Inspection**	**Re-Inspection**	**<3 years**	**3-10 years**	**>10 years**
Motorcycle & Scooter	S$20.71	S$10.36	Nil	Annually	Annually
Additional Test Required:	S$2.18				
Hydrocarbon Emission Test					
*(Motorcycle registered on or after 1 Jul 2003)**					
Classic Motorcycle Seal Inspection	S$11.99	S$11.99	Nil	Nil	Biennially
Car (Internal Combustion Engine or Electric)	S$68.67	S$34.34	Nil	Biennially	Annually
Additional Test Required:	S$7.63				
High Idle Emission Test					
*(Petrol Vehicle registered on or after 1 April 2014)**					
Hydrocarbon Emission Test					
*(Petrol Vehicle registered before 1 April 2014)**	S$2.18				
Diesel Smoke Test	S$21.80	S$21.80			
Compressed Natural Gas (CNG) Inspection	S$14.17	S$14.17			
Off Peak Car (OPC) Seal Inspection	S$11.99	S$11.99	Annually	Annually	Annually
Classic Car Seal Inspection	S$11.99	S$11.99	Nil	Nil	Biennially

(Continued)

Table 1.1. *(Continued)*

Vehicle Category	Inspection Fees		Inspection Frequency		
	Inspection	Re-Inspection	<3 years	3-10 years	>10 years
Private Hire Vehicle Car (PHV) / Tuition Car	S$68.67	S$34.34	Annually	Annually	6-mthly
Additional Test Required:	S$7.63				
High Idle Emission Test					
*(Petrol Vehicle registered on or after 1 April 2014)**					
Hydrocarbon Emission Test	S$2.18				
*(Petrol Vehicle registered before 1 April 2014)**					
Diesel Smoke Test	S$21.80	S$21.80			
Private Hire Vehicle Car Decal Inspection	S$11.99	S$11.99	Annually	Annually	6-mthly
Other Vehicle Type					
Light Goods Vehicle *(G Plate)*	S$68.67	S$34.34	Annually	Annually	6-mthly
Additional Test Required:	S$7.63				
High Idle Emission Test					
*(Petrol Vehicle registered on or after 1 April 2014)**					
Hydrocarbon Emission Test	S$2.18				
*(Petrol Vehicle registered before 1 April 2014)**					
Diesel Smoke Test *(Light Goods Vehicle)*	S$21.80	S$21.80			
Heavy Goods Vehicle / Bus	S$80.66	S$40.33	Annually	Annually	6-mthly
(2 Axles. E.g P, Y Plate)					

Heavy Goods Vehicle / Bus	S$87.20	S$46.87			
(>2 Axles. E.g P, X Plate)					
Additional Test Required:	S$32.70	S$32.70			
Diesel Smoke Test					
(Heavy Goods Vehicle and Bus)					
Trailer	S$68.67	S$34.34	Annually	Annually	Annually
Taxi	S$68.67	S$34.34	Annually	6-mthly	NA
Additional Test Required:	S$7.63				
High Idle Emission Test					
*(Petrol Vehicle registered on or after 1 April 2014)**					
Diesel Smoke Test	S$21.80	S$21.80			
Other Additional Statutory Test Requirements					
New Seal / Re-seal For OPC / Classic Vehicle	S$22.89	N.A.	N.A.	N.A.	N.A.
Airfield Vehicle Inspection	S$21.80	$21.80	N.A.	N.A.	N.A.
Private Hire Vehicle Car Decal Installation and Registration	S$22.67	N.A.	N.A.	N.A.	N.A.

Above fees are inclusive of 9% GST.

Note: From 1 January 2025, all taxis below 3 years old will be required to undergo annual periodic inspections, instead of the previous 6-monthly periodic inspection frequency. All Chauffeured Private Hire Cars above 10 years old will be required to undergo 6-monthly periodic inspections, instead of the previous annual periodic inspection frequency. For more information, please click here.

Source: https://www.vicom.com.sg/Our-Services/Vehicle-Inspection/Inspection-Price-and-Schedule-List

The vehicular testing business commands a 70% market share in Singapore. In Singapore, there are two main players in the vehicular testing business, namely Vicom and STA Inspection. Vicom has seven locations while STA Inspection has only two locations. Therefore, Vicom owns 78% of the vehicle inspection centres in Singapore. Vehicles have to be sent for inspection as per the schedule below. The fees are also shown.

Vicom is 67.51% owned by ComfortDelGro. As you may know, ComfortDelGro owns the largest taxi fleet in Singapore. Where would ComfortDelGro send its taxis for inspection? There are no prizes for guessing.

In 2009, a $4.7 million Vehicle Emission Testing Laboratory (VETL) was set up ($2.3 million was forked out by Land Transport Authority). The VETL is the first of its kind being set up in the region and is compliant with Euro V standard. The centre will be a boon especially to parallel importers, many of which have had difficulty meeting a new fuel-efficiency labelling scheme that became mandatory in April 2009. Testing had to be done at independent labs in Japan or Hong Kong, the nearest places with such testing facilities. Prior to this, parallel importers had to send their cars to Hong Kong for testing, costing around $4000.

The vehicular inspection and assessment business contributed 31.1% of FY2011's revenues. 60.7% of the revenue was contributed by the non-vehicular testing and inspection business, Setsco. 8.2% of the revenue was contributed by other related businesses.

Setsco is one of Singapore's largest testing and inspection companies. It serves a wide spectrum of industries such as electronics, biotechnology, aerospace, marine and offshore, oil and petrochemical, engineering and construction. It is operating in a competitive industry. However, despite the competition, high barrier of entry exists as companies have to meet the high accreditation standards and government body approvals like SAC-SINGLAS and CAAS SAR-145 certification. The whole list of accreditation can be found at http://www.setsco.com/accred.htm.

Also, once one is able to secure a steady base of customers, recurring income is expected as these services may need to be performed on a regular basis. Switching cost may also be high as labels and certificates need to be changed and the products already certified previously need to be re-certified.

Future Catalysts

The government has capped the vehicle growth rate at 0.5% from February 2013 to January 2015. This means there will be increasing COE prices. This in turn means lesser new cars will be bought and more older cars on the roads, needing inspection regularly. This translates to increasing revenue for Vicom.

In 2012, Government Budget, the government announced the "Bus Services Enhancement Fund" where 800 buses will be added by 2016. With more buses, there will be an increase in revenue for Vicom. Being diesel operated, they will also have to undergo Chassis Dynamometer Smoke Test (CDST) for an extra $26 (before GST). It is an increase in recurring income for Vicom since public buses have to be inspected every six months.

Also, come 2014, Singapore will adopt the Euro V standard for diesel vehicles. To encourage the adoption of new and cleaner diesel technologies, the Special Tax for Euro V-compliant cars will be lowered from $1.25 per cubic centimetre (cc) of engine capacity to $0.40 per cc from January 2013 — a reduction of 68 per cent from the rate charged for Euro IV cars. When such diesel vehicles are sent for inspection, an extra $17 (before GST) for CDST inspection has to be paid to Vicom. Also, more parallel importers may start to import Euro V compliant diesel car models with the tax rebates. These cars have to be certified, under the Mandatory Fuel Economy Labelling Scheme, which only VETL can support, bringing in more revenue for Vicom.

With the construction boom in Singapore running well into the future to support the increasing population, Setsco is set to benefit with increasing construction materials and products sent for testing.

Financials

- Consistently increasing revenue and net profits
  - Revenue grew from $46.9 million to $97.1 million. That's a CAGR of 9.5%.
  - Net Profit grew from $7.68 million to $26.4 million, translating into a CAGR of 16.7%.
- Gross, operating and net profit margins that are either increasing or kept steady
  - Gross Margins grew from 89.14% in 2004 to 93.9% in 2011.
  - Operating Margin grew from 24.6% in 2004 to 32.5% in 2012.
  - Net Profit Margin grew from 16.38% in 2004 to 27.2% in 2012.
- Very conservative Cash and Debt level
  - Vicom has had a debt-free balance sheet since 2005 and is flush with cash.
- High ROE and ROA
- Superior FCF
- Increasing dividends
  - Dividends per share have increased from $0.0575 in 2004 to $0.182 in 2012. That's a 216% increase!

Valuation

In case you have forgotten the important figures, we need for Relative Valuation work, they are as follows:

- Historical Net Income compounded annual growth rate: 16.7%
- Estimate Net Income compounded annual growth rate in the next five years: 10%
- Current Share Count: 88.35 million
- Estimated future Share Count: 91.75 million (share count grew at a compounded rate of 0.7% per year from 2004 to 2012)
- Current Net Income: $26.41 million

	FY2004	FY2005	FY2006	FY2007	FY2008	FY2009	FY2010	FY2011	FY2012
Revenue (S$ '000)	46,894	49,192	56,937	64,747	73,845	77,953	83,978	90,739	97,102
Gross Profit (S$ '000)	41,800	45,000	50,200	56,900	65,400	72,100	77,978	85,200	
Gross Profit Margin (%)	89.14	91.48	88.17	87.88	88.56	92.49	92.86	93.90	0.00
Operating Profit (S$ '000)	11,538	11,344	13,352	16,762	19,828	24,551	26,896	29,986	31,572
Operating Margin (%)	24.60	23.06	23.45	25.89	26.85	31.49	32.03	33.05	32.51
Net Profit (S$ '000)	7,683	8,658	10,295	13,500	15,794	20,037	22,165	25,100	26,409
Net Profit Margin (%)	16.38	17.60	18.08	20.85	21.39	25.70	26.39	27.66	27.20
Diluted No. of Shares Outstanding ('000)	83,166	83,459	84,066	85,056	85,098	85,896	86,616	87,613	88,352
Cash and cash equivalents (S$ '000)	8,068	9,526	13,710	14,015	27,691	42,377	49,083	55,010	65,991
Total Debt (S$ '000)	2,417	0	0	0	0	0	0	0	0
Current Ratio	1.022	1.379	1.512	1.352	1.805	2.181	2.486	2.568	3.010
ROE (%)	14.53	14.95	16.72	23.21	23.39	25.29	24.10	23.80	22.66
ROA (%)	10.92	11.78	13.08	17.26	17.47	19.12	18.75	18.74	18.22
Shareholder's Equity (S$ '000)	52,863	57,931	61,562	58,156	67,518	79,240	91,990	105,457	116,545
Cashflow from Ops (S$ '000)	12,264	13,002	16,453	19,670	24,827	29,478	27,509	30,308	30,659
Capex (S$ '000)	1,556	2,306	5,604	2,372	4,452	7,915	11,092	12,155	4,627
Free Cash Flow (S$ '000)	10,708	10,696	10,849	17,298	20,375	21,563	16,417	18,153	26,032
Gross Dividends (SG cents)	5.75	6.50	7.65	5.75	9.25	11.80	12.90	14.40	15.00
Special Dividends (SG cents)	0.00	2.00	7.00	12.50	0.00	0.00	3.20	3.20	3.20
Total Dividends (SG cents)	5.75	8.50	14.65	18.25	9.25	11.80	16.10	17.60	18.20

- Estimated Net Income five years into the future: $42.53 million
- Earnings Per Share five years into the future: $0.4635 million
- Estimated PE ratio five years into the future: 12–15
- Estimated Share Price five years into the future: $5.56–6.95
- Discount Rate: 15%
- Intrinsic Value: **$2.76–3.45**

For the DCF method, the relevant figures are as follows:

- Historical FCF Growth: 11.7%
- Estimated FCF Growth for the next 10 years: 10%
- Terminal Growth Rate: 3%
- Current FCF: $26.03 million
- Sum of future FCF discounted back to the present: $374.812 million
- Current Share Count: 88.35 million
- Intrinsic Value: **$4.24**

Did we miss out on anything? If you answered: Margin of Safety, then well done! So yes, if we apply a Margin of Safety of 15% to our estimates of intrinsic value coming from the two methods, we obtain intrinsic values of: **$2.35–2.93** and **$3.60.**

Kingsmen Creatives

Overview of Kingsmen Creatives

Kingsmen was founded in 1976 by Benedict Soh and Simon Ong. The company has four business segments, namely: Exhibitions & Museums, Retail & Corporate Interiors, Research & Design, and Alternative Marketing. To put in clearer terms, Kingsmen is involved in designing and fitting out of retail shops; creating permanent and temporary installations for theme parks, events and exhibition spaces; and providing brand activation for companies, among others. Its clients include famous brands such as Audi, BMW Chanel, Esprit, Hublot, Swarovski, Tag Heuer, Universal Studios Singapore and Hong Kong Disneyland. The company has an international presence with 18 full-service offices across Asia and the Middle East, and worldwide affiliates.

It is often said that this business has low barriers to entry. This is true. However, even though the barriers to entry are low, the "reputational" barriers are high. Kingsmen has a strong brand name in the industry and has many blue-chip clients to its name. The relationship it has built with its clients over the years cannot be easily prised away by new competitors that offer lower prices. As you know, when it comes to building a personal relationship, it takes time to foster a strong relationship, to understand one another and to trust one another. Kingsmen's clients would prefer to go back to Kingsmen for future projects since both parties understand each others' working habits and norms. Therefore, the stickiness is there. In fact, 70% of Kingsmen's clients are repeat customers. Clients returning to Kingsmen is analogous to how most patients go back to the same doctor when they are unwell, as they trust that the doctor to cure the illness. On the part of its clients, they would not want to trade quality, provided by Kingsmen, for a lower price, provided by an untested competitor, as the brand equity of their brands is at stake. Also, during tough times like an economic downturn, clients select companies which they know will not disappear overnight, which would otherwise cause a bigger "headache" with half-done fixtures and fit-outs.

Kingsmen also has vast experience in this field since 1976. The track record speaks for itself. Its repeat clients as well as new ones choosing Kingsmen for its first foray into Singapore, like H&M and Abercrombie & Fitch, are a testament of the high-quality work provided by Kingsmen.

Kingsmen has full-service facilities to provide "one-stop-shop" solutions to its clients. Benedict Soh, one of its founders and Kingsmen's Executive Chairman, explained during an interview what it means by "one-stop-shop": "When an international retailer plans to enter Asia by setting up five stores across five countries, the retailer only has to work with the Kingsmen team at one single office at one single geographical point. Thereafter, Kingsmen will manufacture the fixtures and roll them out in the different stores. Our competitive edge lies in bringing convenience and cost savings to the clients."

To witness the extreme quality of the interior fit-outs done by Kingsmen, one can visit retail shops like Malmaison by The Hour Glass. The project was named the "Best Retail Concept of the Year" during the Singapore Retailers Association Awards 2011. One can also pay a visit to Universal Studios Singapore where Kingsmen built Shrek's House, Shrek's Castle and Romeo Drive, among others (don't forget to enjoy the trilling rides while you are there!).

Management

The founders, Benedict Soh and Simon Ong, are currently the Executive Chairman and Group Managing Director respectively. They have more than 80 years of combined experience in the field!

The founders and the company have also won many awards. The list of awards won can be seen from their website at http://www.kingsmen-int.com/awards-and-affiliations/. The most commendable award won was by Benedict Soh when he was accorded the "Lifetime Achievement for Outstanding Contribution to Tourism" by the Singapore Tourism Board recently.

Mr. Soh and Mr. Ong both own 24.6% of the company each and they have not sold any of their shares since Day One. This shows that they believe in what they are doing and believe in the company they founded. The high ownership of shares by the founders ensures that their interests are aligned with that of the minority shareholders.

Risks

The first risk is that of talents. Since this business is talent-based and has low barriers to entry, any experienced staff from Kingsmen can resign and easily start a similar business. Talent drain is given. However, the mid to high-tier market segments and international clients Kingsmen serves means that small local players cannot compete against Kingsmen. The company also has a strong corporate culture to minimize the push factors that makes a talent move away from Kingsmen. The company creates a conducive working environment for its staff, has "makan" and bonding sessions every month in the main office and regular in-house design competitions to promote healthy competition and to upgrade the skills of the designers. It also organises fun activities through it Sports and Recreation Club and also training programmes like Outward Bound School for its staff to discover their strengths and weaknesses and bond with one another. In *Pulses* magazine published in September 2010, it was quoted that someone whom Mr Ong met recently likened the group's working culture to Apple and its competitors Microsoft. Furthermore, shares of Kingsmen are issued as incentives to employees so that they have an attachment to the company. Overseas offices are not exempted from this share scheme. They, too, are offered shares so that they have a sense of belonging with the Group.

The second risk is that of the economic cycle. If a crisis were to happen, the exhibition division may be affected. Clients may cut down on their expenditure for exhibitions. However, as Kingsmen also has its interior business, it is less reliant on any one industry. Unless the down cycle of the economy is protracted, there should not be much harm to Kingsmen's business.

The third risk is that of competitors. Kingsmen has a major competitor in the form of Pico, which is listed in Hong Kong. Pico is big in the theme park and exhibition sector. However, for huge projects like major theme park projects, everyone gets a slice, including Kingsmen.

That was what happened during the Universal Studios Singapore (USS) project where both Pico and Kingsmen were heavily involved in the project.

Pico has an entrenched position in China. It may be hard for Kingsmen to gain increased market share in that region. On the other hand, Kingmen is huge in the interior sector with many blue-chip clients and established relationship, whereas Pico is not big in this segment.

Catalyst

Singapore is seeing a tourism boom due to the new USS theme park and casinos. The Meetings, Incentives, Conventions & Exhibitions (MICE) sector is also burgeoning. Furthermore, many tourists are coming here exclusively to shop.

More international brands are setting up shop in Singapore but there is room for more growth. Only 38.9% of international brands have presence here in Singapore (*Source*: CBRE — "How Global Is the Business of Retail" 2012). In 2011, H&M and Abercrombie & Fitch opened their flagship stores here. These international brands see Singapore as a springboard to expand into Southeast Asia.

There are also many theme parks slated to open in the region. Kingsmen has experience in this segment after undertaking the major USS project back in 2009. Current theme parks have to undergo sprucing up and this creates more opportunities for Kingsmen as well.

Retail malls in Orchard Road and also in the suburban have to be spruced by asset enhancement initiatives regularly to entice shoppers. Also, during the festive periods every year, retail outlets refurbish their outlets and all these bode well for Kingsmen. More suburban malls like Seletar Mall, Bedok Mall and Westgate will be coming up and some of Kingsmen's clients like H&M are setting up shop in such malls. More international brands may follow suit to prevent overcrowding of Orchard Road.

Kingsmen is also enjoying growing demand for its store fixtures, which it exports to its retail clients in the US and Europe.

Kingsmen was featured in 9th January 2010 edition of The Edge magazine. In it, Mr. Soh said he predicts the company can double its top line in the next five years due to the export market and the potential to expand its business in the 18 countries in which it operates. Kingsmen is selective about the job it undertakes to ensure all the work it takes on actually contributes to the bottom line instead of just focusing on expanding top line, which is easy. He also sees growth in Indonesia as foreign brands are slowly entering the fray. Benedict added that there is plenty of growth potential in China and Middle East as the markets there are huge.

Financials

- Consistently increasing revenue and net profits
    - Revenue grew from $63.3 million to $290.3 million. That's a CAGR of 21%.
    - Net Profit grew from $1.26 million to $17.12 million, translating into a CAGR of 38.6%.
- Gross, operating and net profit margins that are either increasing or kept steady
    - Gross Margins have kept steady around 25% to 31% from 2004 to 2012.
    - Operating Margin grew from 24.6% in 2004 to 32.5% in 2012.
    - Net Profit Margin grew from 16.38% in 2004 to 27.2% in 2012.
- Very conservative Cash and Debt level
    - Kingsmen has very low debt compared to its cash levels.
- High ROE and ROA
- Superior FCF
- Increasing dividends

Valuation

The important figures we need for Relative Valuation work are as follows:

- Historical Net Income compounded annual growth rate: 38.55%
- Estimate Net Income compounded annual growth rate in the next five years: 12%
- Current Share Count: 191.43 million
- Estimated future Share Count: 222.63 million (share count grew at a compounded rate of 3.06% per year from 2004 to 2012)
- Current Net Income: $17.123 million
- Estimated Net Income five years into the future: $30.18 million
- Earnings Per Share five years into the future: $0.1356
- Estimated PE ratio five years into the future: 12–15
- Estimated Share Price five years into the future: $1.63 to $2.03
- Discount Rate: 15%
- Intrinsic Value: **$0.81–1.01**
- Margin of Safety: 15%, therefore adjusted Intrinsic Value = $0.689–0.86

For the DCF method, the relevant figures are as follows:

- Historical FCF Growth: 33.6%
- Estimated FCF Growth for the next 10 years: 15%
- Terminal Growth Rate: 3%
- Current FCF: $28.335 million
- Sum of future FCF discounted back to the present: $554.894 million
- Current Share Count: 191.43 million
- Intrinsic Value: **$2.90**
- Margin of Safety: 15%, therefore adjusted Intrinsic Value = $2.465

Kingsmen Creatives	FY2004	FY2005	FY2006	FY2007	FY2008	FY2009	FY2010	FY2011	FY2012
Revenue (S$ '000)	63,261	76,742	108,945	146,131	190,554	242,036	233,631	260,988	290,310
Gross Profit (S$ '000)	16,467	20,541	27,784	39,720	58,533	59,542	63,877	66,665	72,578
Gross Profit Margin (%)	26.03	26.77	25.50	27.18	30.72	24.60	27.34	25.54	25.00
Operating Profit (S$ '000)	1,632	2,752	5,842	12,152	18,734	18,583	19,519	19,184	15,827
Operating Margin (%)	2.58	3.59	5.36	8.32	9.83	7.68	8.35	7.35	5.45
Net Profit (S$ '000)	1,261	2,192	4,937	9,365	14,176	14,900	15,066	16,327	17,123
Net Profit Margin (%)	1.99	2.86	4.53	6.41	7.44	6.16	6.45	6.26	5.90
Diluted No. of Shares Outstanding (adjusted for 3-for-2 stock split on 2008)	150,351	151,641	151,641	178,560	190,034	189,381	189,872	190,699	191,434
Cash and cash equivalents (S$ '000)	3,161	5,710	6,546	21,483	28,151	22,827	29,903	33,231	53,081
Total Debt (S$ '000)	453	944	1,699	1,657	1,438	1,291	5,290	5,205	4,645
Current Ratio	1.43	1.325	1.302	1.31	1.322	1.40	1.45	1.49	1.55
ROE (%)	9.62	14.90	26.66	26.19	33.19	28.72	26.41	24.96	23.12
ROA (%)	4.27	5.01	8.48	9.45	13.03	10.79	10.35	9.86	9.53
Shareholder's Equity (S$ '000)	13,108	14,708	18,520	35,756	42,706	51,876	57,056	65,418	74,057
Cashflow from Ops (S$ '000)	3,282	5,641	9,022	12,852	25,761	1,381	20,317	12,853	30,410
Capex (S$ '000)	490	1,422	1,172	766	11,210	1,362	6,152	2,778	2,075
Free Cash Flow (S$ '000)	2,792	4,219	7,850	12,086	14,551	19	14,165	10,075	28,335
Gross Dividends (SG cents)	0.70	1.00	1.50	2.00	3.00	3.50	3.50	4.00	4.00
Special Dividends (SG cents)	0.00	0.00	0.50	1.00	0.00	0.00	0.50	0.00	0.00
Total Dividends (SG cents)	0.70	1.00	2.00	3.00	3.00	3.50	4.00	4.00	4.00

Super Group

Overview of Super Group

Super Group is well-known for its 3-in-1 instant coffeemix, especially in Singapore and Asia. It is the only company in Singapore and the region with the manufacturing capability for instant coffee, instant cereals and non-dairy products. Super has a distribution reach of over 50 countries and it is one of the top three market leaders in the South-east Asian markets. According to AC Nielsen, Super has a market share of about 37% in Singapore, 13% in Malaysia and above 30% in both Myanmar and Thailand.

The group has more than 300 products such as instant coffee and tea, instant cereal, flavoured can drinks, cup noodles and potato chips. Its products are manufactured under stringent conditions in accordance to ISO 22000 and HACCP certifications.

The group has an ingredients division that sold products to the top five milk tea players in China. This division was started in 2005 to have vertical integration to better control the quality of raw materials. Half the ingredients are produced for internal usage while the rest are sold to external parties. This allowed Super to move into the business-to-business segment. Having started off to ensure consistency in its coffee products, the ingredients unit has since morphed into an immense source of revenue for the firm.

Super has 14 state-of-the-art manufacturing plants located in Singapore, Malaysia, Myanmar, Thailand and China. The sophisticated facilities provide barriers to entry to potential competitors. The highly automated facility also reduces manpower costs and provides high-quality product control. Its plants also have a successful system in place which gives the instant coffee the aroma of a freshly brewed cup. The plants are also scalable to double the annual production volume for ingredients.

With manufacturing plants in the region, it is able to localise itself in various markets. This means making different blends of its instant coffee mixes for different markets and packaging them differently.

For example, the Thais prefer their coffee sweeter so Super produces sweeter coffee there. While in Singapore, Singaporeans prefer lesser sugar. In Myanmar, Super recently came up with a sachet that has sugar on one side, separated from the coffee and creamer on the other side, so drinkers choose their own sweetness level.

Super Group continues to invent new products and packaging designs and it can do so efficiently due to its regionalisation strategy. For example, recently in Malaysia, the company took just six to eight months to roll out a new product — the "Super Power" range of five-in-one coffees, which are a blend of its white coffee mix with added ingredients like tongat ali, collagen and ginseng.

Super has also won numerous awards including the Brand Laureate "Best Brand in Food and Beverage — Coffee" and "Best Brand Category, Brand Communication — Coffee" in 2009 for consecutive years. It also won Finance Brands Award's "Singapore Top 100 Brands" in 2010.

The company opened Owl Cafe at The Star Vista Mall in September 2012. It opened a cafe mainly to increase brand awareness. Super did a rebranding exercise in January 2013 with a refreshed logo. The company surely knows the benefits of re-branding, having done a successful exercise in 2007. In that year, it re-packaged its Ipoh White Coffee and sales shot up 12-fold! It has roped in celebrities in the past like JJ Lin to promote its coffee line.

Management

Management is competent. This can be seen from the regionalisation strategy and having ventured into the ingredients business after having perceived demand for it. The numbers show competency of management too. The management also puts the money where its mouth is. It said it will open a physical store some time back and it has indeed opened one, in the form of "Owl Cafe".

Since it's a family business, there might be things in place to benefit the family members only and solid ideas suggested might not come to pass due to family hierarchy. However, I do not see this as a huge problem as the management has been created high ROE and share buybacks has been done in 2002, 2005, 2008, and 2009 as well. The Teo and Te families own around 30% of the company.

Future Catalysts

Having successfully established the company as a market leader for instant coffee in Asia markets like Malaysia, Thailand, Singapore and Myanmar, Super is looking to increase market penetration in Indonesia's growing instant coffee market by forming a joint venture with Petra Foods. It is also looking increase market penetration in Philippines' instant coffee market with a joint venture with San Miguel. In Vietnam, it has induced trial of products via sampling. Super has a target to be top 4 players in these new markets by 2015.

Financials

- Consistently increasing revenue and net profits
    - Revenue grew from $171.9 million to $519.3 million. That's a CAGR of 14.8%.
    - Net Profit grew from $18.2 million to $79.0 million, translating into a CAGR of 20.1%.
- Gross margins have been falling, but operating margins have kept steady while net profit margins have been increasing
    - Gross Margins have steadily decreased from 42.5% in 2004 to 35% in 2012.
    - Operating Margin grew from 15% in 2004 to 17.3% in 2012.
    - Net Profit Margin grew from 10.59% in 2004 to 15.2% in 2012 (there's a slight cause for concern in terms of net profit margin in 2008, when it hit a low of 8.36%).
- Very conservative Cash and Debt level
    - Supergroup has been debt-free since 2010.

- High ROE and ROA
- Superior FCF
  - We can see that Super Group's FCF took a big tumble in FY2011. The reason was because the company was reinvesting heavily into a new line of business — the Food Ingredients business. Thus, in such a special situation, we could normalise its CapEx for 2011 and 2012. This essentially estimates how CapEx would look like if the reinvestment did not take place. To us, a reasonable estimate of CapEx for 2011 and 2012 would be about $20 million each year. This would bring the estimated FCF for 2011 and 2012 to $38.9 million and $65.7 million respectively.
- Increasing dividends

Valuation

The important figures we need for Relative Valuation work are as follows:

- Historical Net Income compounded annual growth rate: 20.1%
- Estimate Net Income compounded annual growth rate in the next five years: 15%
- Current Share Count: 557.5 million
- Estimated future Share Count: 608.6 million (share count grew at a compounded rate of 1.77% per year from 2004 to 2012)
- Current Net Income: $79.0 million
- Estimated Net Income five years into the future: $158.9 million
- Earnings Per Share five years into the future: $0.261
- Estimated PE ratio five years into the future: 20–25
- Estimated Share Price five years into the future: $5.22 to $6.53
- Discount Rate: 15%
- Intrinsic Value: **$2.60–3.25**
- Margin of Safety: 15%, therefore adjusted Intrinsic Value = $2.21–2.76

Super Group	FY2004	FY2005	FY2006	FY2007	FY2008	FY2009	FY2010	FY2011	FY2012
Revenue (S$ '000)	171,900	187,900	210,700	253,600	300,200	296,262	351,832	440,972	519,268
Gross Profit (S$ '000)	73,000	76,300	75,500	86,400	99,800	103,407	131,402	142,076	181,426
Gross Profit Margin (%)	42.47	40.61	35.83	34.07	33.24	34.90	37.35	32.22	34.94
Operating Profit (S$ '000)	25,792	29,147	31,110	30,907	36,064	41,682	66,299	71,590	89,810
Operating Profit Margin (%)	15.00	15.51	14.77	12.19	12.01	14.07	18.84	16.23	17.30
Net Profit (S$ '000)	18,200	23,300	24,600	29,300	25,100	40,242	58,355	61,898	79,044
Net Profit Margin (%)	10.59	12.40	11.68	11.55	8.36	13.58	16.59	14.04	15.22
Diluted No. of Shares Outstanding ('000)	484,655	493,436	493,243	538,620	542,425	538,043	547,554	557,403	557,495
Cash and cash equivalents (S$ '000)	35,438	22,800	22,900	21,584	25,844	70,476	141,760	122,672	112,194
Total Debt (S$ '000)	2,457	1,900	1,400	5,056	3,396	1,980	0	0	0
Current Ratio	2.11	1.932	1.632	3.033	2.63	3.144	3.142	2.74	2.50
ROE (%)	11.93	13.52	13.18	12.86	10.05	14.52	17.70	16.20	19.81
ROA (%)	8.15	9.27	8.48	9.26	10.07	14.52	13.05	12.32	14.56
Shareholder's Equity (S$ '000)	152,500	172,300	186,700	227,800	249,800	277,231	329,750	382,178	398,917
Cashflow from Ops (S$ '000)	26,400	21,700	5,600	5,200	35,000	66,400	55,416	58,895	85,672
Capex (S$ '000)	9,500	19,100	18,900	11,400	7,300	6,900	14,577	73,076	63,037
Free Cash Flow (S$ '000)	16,900	2,600	−13,300	−6,200	27,700	59,500	40,839	−14,181	22,635
Gross Dividends (SG cents)	0.80	1.60	1.60	1.60	1.60	2.60	5.40	5.80	7.10
Special Dividends (SG cents)	0.40	0.00	0.00	0.00	0.00	0.00	0.00	0.00	0.00
Total Dividends (SG cents)	1.20	1.60	1.60	1.60	1.60	2.60	5.40	5.80	7.10

For the DCF method, the relevant figures are as follows:

- Historical FCF Growth: 18.5% (assuming a normalised FCF figure would be around $65.7 million)
- Estimated FCF Growth for the next 10 years: 15%
- Terminal Growth Rate: 3%
- Current FCF: $65.7 million
- Sum of future FCF discounted back to the present: $1.221 billion
- Current Share Count: 191.43 million
- Intrinsic Value: **$6.38**
- Margin of Safety: 15%, therefore adjusted Intrinsic Value = $5.42

Thomson Medical Centre

Overview of Thomson Medical Centre

Thomson Medical Centre (TMC) is a leading private hospital in Singapore catering to women and children. Located at Thomson Road, walking distance from Novena Church, it provides a comprehensive range of services with focus in Obstetrics and Gynaecology (O&G) and paediatric services. It has since been delisted at the end of 2010. "Remiser King" Peter Lim offered $1.75 a share to buy over Dr Cheng Wei Chen and family's 39.34% stake in Thomson Medical Centre. Dr Cheng is the founder and largest shareholder of TMC. We are including TMC, even though it has been delisted, to have a case-in-point that fundamentally strong companies do well in the long term, in terms of share price appreciation.

TMC has a wide moat as it had the highest number of live births among all the private hospitals in 2008. The number of babies delivered in TMC in FY2009 was 8,907. The number of total live births in Singapore in 2008 was 39,826 (obtained from Singapore Statistics website). This shows that TMC's share is around 20% and that is significant. The number of births in FY2009 was also the record number of births in TMC and it was breaking its own record year after year from 2008 to 2009.

TMC has VIP rooms and premier wards that make TMC look like a 5-star hotel. Many celebrities have chosen TMC to deliver their babies. 32.2% of the customers are repeat customers. This shows how much people value TMC and the services provided by TMC. It has become a brand name amongst people.

TMC has also won many awards including being in the top position in Customer Satisfaction Index in the healthcare sector in January 2010 and it was one of the five Singapore-listed companies to win the Forbes "Asia's Best 200 Under A Billion" award in September 2009.

Sudhan did some scuttlebutting at TMC back in 2009. He went for a hospital tour that they have regularly to show would-be mothers around the hospital. What he liked about TMC is the fact that they organise hospital tours and care to explain about the various facilities available in TMC. They even showed the operating theatre where water birth can be done. Another thing he noticed about the hospital was that it was rather "crampy" in the aisles and it seemed like the hospital was bursting at the seams. The ground floor seemed cluttered as well. This can be seen as a positive thing at it shows that TMC is a popular hospital. Having said that, the space constraint could be easily mitigated as it had a huge cash hoard to expand the hospital at nearby areas.

Management

Executive chairman, Dr Cheng Wei Chen has 36.19% ownership of TMC. It was stated in the IPO prospectus that TMC will look into overseas venture and did just that with Vietnam venture. The management did what it promised.

Financials

By now, you might have noticed very similar characteristics in the Numbers of these few companies we have shared. And it is not by coincidence! — these are mostly the kind of figures we would like to see in companies that we invest in.

With regard to TMC, this is what we see:

- Consistently increasing revenue and net profits
    - o Revenue grew from $31.3 million to $81.7 million. That's a CAGR of 17.3%.
    - o Net Profit grew from $4.17 million to $16.25 million, translating into a CAGR of 25.4%.
- Gross, operating and net profit margins that are either increasing or kept steady
    - o Gross Margins have steadily increased from 40.8% in 2004 to 43.7% in 2012.
    - o Operating Margin grew even more: from 19.1% to 24.3%.
    - o Net Profit Margins had the most impressive growth (remember how we discussed in The Numbers about the importance of growing margins?). It grew from 13.3% in 2004 to 19.9% in 2012.
- Very conservative Cash and Debt level
    - o TMC started out with almost four times as much debt as cash but improved its Cash vs Debt ratio very quickly due to its prodigious FCF generation. Soon, the company was in a very comfortable position with regard to Cash and Debt levels.
- High ROE and ROA
- Superior FCF
- Increasing dividends

Valuation

Thomson Medical Centre is a special case as it is now a private company. But, we will still go through the valuation exercise, to see how investors in the company would have thought about it at that time.

As always, let's list the important figures we need for Relative Valuation work:

- Historical Net Income compounded annual growth rate: 25.4%.
- Estimate Net Income compounded annual growth rate in the next five years: 20%.

	FY2004	FY2005	FY2006	FY2007	FY2008	FY2009	FY2010
Revenue (S$ '000)	31,312	41,176	46,513	52,361	60,264	67,394	81,678
Gross Profit (S$ '000)	12,769	17,399	19,670	22,631	26,571	29,082	35,703
Gross Profit Margin (%)	40.78	42.26	42.29	43.22	44.09	43.15	43.71
Operating Profit (S$ '000)	5,970	7,794	9,364	11,790	14,067	15,827	19,882
Operating Profit Margin (%)	19.07	18.93	20.13	22.52	23.34	23.48	24.34
Net Profit (S$ '000)	4,174	5,329	6,771	9,501	11,155	12,715	16,251
Net Profit Margin (%)	13.33	12.94	14.56	18.15	18.51	18.87	19.90
Diluted No. of Shares Outstanding (adjusted for the 10-for-1 bonus share issue on Aug 2006)	218,874	261,643	291,977	291,977	293,071	292,125	295,345
Cash and cash equivalents (S$ '000)	7,854	10,976	14,046	15,288	6,079	9,841	17,485
Total Debt (S$ '000)	29,700	11,160	9,800	8,440	4,080	2,720	1,360
Current Ratio	1.061	1.338	1.442	1.254	1.272	1.388	1.803
ROE (%)	8.39	7.56	8.63	10.24	10.19	11.42	11.4
ROA (%)	4.63	5.72	6.66	8.15	8.54	9.61	9.7
Shareholder's Equity (S$ '000)	49,767	70,486	78,442	92,769	109,495	111,303	142,100
Cashflow from Ops (S$ '000)	5,387	9,610	11,518	13,604	14,031	19,141	20,844
Capex (S$ '000)	1,907	1,507	3,134	5,179	3,265	5,329	808
Free Cash Flow (S$ '000)	3,480	8,103	8,384	8,425	10,766	13,812	20,036
Gross Dividends (SG cents)	N.A	1.00	1.28	1.00	2.50	2.50	3.20
Special Dividends (SG cents)	N.A	0.00	0.45	0.75	0.00	0.30	0.00
Total Dividends (SG cents)	N.A	1.00	1.73	1.75	2.50	2.80	3.20

- Current Share Count: 295.3 million.
- Estimated future Share Count: 379.1 million (share count grew at a compounded rate of 5.1% per year from 2004 to 2010)
- Current Net Income: $16.25 million
- Estimated Net Income five years into the future: $40.4 million
- Earnings Per Share five years into the future: $0.1066
- Estimated PE ratio five years into the future: 20–25
- Estimated Share Price five years into the future: $2.13 to $2.67
- Discount Rate: 15%
- Intrinsic Value: **$1.06–1.33**
- Margin of Safety: 15%, therefore adjusted Intrinsic Value = $0.90–1.13

For the DCF method, the relevant figures are as follows:

- Historical FCF Growth: 33.9%
- Estimated FCF Growth for the next 10 years: 20%
- Terminal Growth Rate: 3%
- Current FCF: $20.0 million
- Sum of future FCF discounted back to the present: $518.3 million
- Current Share Count: 295.3 million
- Intrinsic Value: **$1.76**
- Margin of Safety: 15%, therefore adjusted Intrinsic Value = $1.49

**Note that TMC was taken private at a price of $1.75 per share in end 2010.

Duolingo

Overview of Duolingo

Duolingo is a language learning app that makes learning a new language fun and approachable. It uses gamification to deliver bite-sized lessons with interactive quizzes and activities to users.

The key features of Duolingo include free-to-use, mobile-friendly, personalised learning and bite-sized lessons. Users can use the app for free or they can choose to pay a subscription fee to remove advertisements within the app. Duolingo users access the app via their smartphones, making this mode of learning easily accessible to users across the globe. Users receive personalised notifications and learning roadmaps to help them achieve their learning objectives. Last but not least, the bite-sized lessons include interactive quizzes for users to track their learning progress and cover reading, writing, and speaking.

Duolingo was founded in 2011 by Luis von Ahn, a computer science professor at Carnegie Mellon University, and Severin Hacker, von Ahn's graduate student. They shared a common vision of making language learning fun, engaging, and accessible. By combining gamification with a focus on learning practical language skills, Duolingo introduced a spaced repetition system to reinforce language learning.

As of the second quarter of 2024, Duolingo has around 34 million monthly active users. It generated US$531 million in revenue in 2023. What is worth mentioning is that only 8.6% of Duolingo's users are paying users and only 8% of revenue comes from advertisements. This means that less than 10% of Duolingo's users contributed to more than 80% of Duolingo's revenue.

Duolingo has two streams of revenue, which are (1) the paid tier, where users pay a monthly subscription to remove advertisements and get unlimited lives, and (2) advertisements, which are typically shown to users towards the end of a lesson.

Management

As mentioned, Duolingo is founded by Luis von Ahn and Severin Hacker. Currently, von Ahn serves as CEO and Board Chairman, while Hacker is the Chief Technical Officer (CTO).

Prior to founding Duolingo, von Ahn created reCAPTCHA, a system that used CAPTCHAs to digitize books. With this success, von Ahn and Hacker managed to get funding from the MacArthur Fellowship and a National Science Foundation grant to kickstart Duolingo.

Duolingo's current management team also comprises experienced individuals such as Robert Meese as Chief Business Officer, Molly Linsay as Chief People Officer, and Matthew Skaruppa as Chief Financial Officer.

Future Catalysts

There are three main catalysts for Duolingo's growth: (1) AI notifications, (2) Duolingo's Max Tier, a premium subscription tier which allows users to role-play with AI-powered bots, and (3) expansion to new markets and languages.

AI notifications and AI-powered A/B testing have already been implemented in the existing Duolingo app. By leveraging AI, Duolingo's AI notifications are able to test for the best possible way to engage users, so as to get them to keep coming back to the app to learn. For example, Duolingo's AI team tests the length of the notification message, how it is being crafted, and the time of the day to send notifications to users.

Duolingo Max Tier is priced at US$30 per month. It allows users to practice their speaking and writing with an AI bot anytime they wish. This reduces users' fear of being judged by a human tutor or practice buddy.

Lastly, Duolingo continues to expand its product offering to new markets and language offerings.

Financials

- Consistently increasing revenue
    - o Revenue grew from US$70.8 million to US$689.5 million. That's a CAGR of 61.5%.

Duolingo	*2019	2020	2021	2022	2023	LTM as of 30 Sep 2024
Revenue (US$ '000)	70,760	161,696	250,772	369,495	531,109	689,459
Gross Profit (US$ '000)	50,023	115,709	181,586	270,064	389,004	504,168
Gross Profit Margin (%)	70.69	71.56	72.41	73.09	73.24	73.13
Operating Profit (US$ '000)	–14,125	–16,011	–60,007	–65,195	–13,259	17,400
Operating Profit Margin (%)	–19.96	–9.90	–23.93	–17.64	–2.50	2.52
Net Profit (US$ '000)	–13,554	–15,776	–60,135	–59,574	16,067	86,784
Net Profit Margin (%)	–19.15	–9.76	–23.98	–16.12	3.03	12.59
Diluted No. of Shares Outstanding ('000)	—	—	23,433	39,470	46,522	47,515
Cash and cash equivalents (US$ '000)	59,843	120,490	553,922	608,180	747,610	854,409
Total Debt (US$ '000)	0	0	0	0	0	0
Current Ratio	2.46	2.41	5.20	3.84	3.24	3.09
ROE (%)	—	N.A.	N.A.	N.A.	2.68%	12.08%
ROA (%)	—	N.A.	N.A.	N.A.	1.89%	8.30%
Shareholder's Equity (US$ '000)	–83,976	–80,691	513,056	542,078	655,501	822,453
Cashflow from Ops (US$ '000)	2,152	17,708	9,170	53,656	153,614	251,362
Capex (US$ '000)	5,246	4,014	6,206	10,124	13,684	22,848
Free Cash Flow (US$ '000)	–3,094	13,694	2,964	43,532	139,930	228,514

Note: *Duolingo IPO-ed only in July 2021, so its historical financials go back only to 2019.

- Gross margins have been steadily rising, as has the operating margin
    - Gross Margin steadily increased from 70.7% in 2019 to 73.1% in the 12 months through to 30 September 2024.
    - Operating Margin increased from –20% to 2.5%.
- Duolingo turned profitable in 2023 and produced a Net Profit Margin of 12.6% in the 12 months through to 30 September 2024.
- Duolingo's diluted share count increased by 17.9% in 2023, which is an undesirably high rate of dilution, but the diluted share count as of 30 September 2024 is only 2.1% higher than the 2023 figure, which is acceptable.
- Very conservative Cash and Debt level
    - Duolingo has been debt-free since at least 2019.
- Duolingo's ROE rose to a decent mid-teens level in the 12 months through to 30 September 2024
- Superior FCF
    - Duolingo's free cash flow has increased five-fold since 2022 and by comparing its free cash flow to its revenue, it's clear that the company is converting a healthy chunk of its revenue into free cash flow.

Valuation

The important figures we need for Relative Valuation work are as follows:

- Historical revenue compounded annual growth rate: 61.5%
- Estimated revenue compounded annual growth rate in the next five years: 30%
- Current Share Count: 47.515 million
- Estimated future Share Count: 55.08 million (this assumes a 3% compounded annual growth rate in the number of shares over five years, which is higher than the 2.1% increase in the diluted share count from the end of 2023 to 30 September 2024)

- Current Revenue: US$689.5 million
- Estimated Revenue five years into the future:US$2,558.2 million (this uses the estimated compounded annual growth of 30% mentioned above)
- Estimated Net Income five years into the future: US$639.6 million (this assumes Duolingo's net profit margin expands to 25%)
- Earnings Per Share five years into the future: US$11.61
- Estimated PE ratio five years into the future: 30–35
- Estimated Share Price five years into the future: $348 to $406
- Discount Rate: 15%
- Intrinsic Value: **$173–202**
- Margin of Safety: 15%, therefore adjusted Intrinsic Value = $147–172

For the DCF method, the relevant figures are as follows:

- Historical FCF Growth: 157.9% (this is calculated with the FCF figures for 2022 and the 12 months ended 30 September 2024)
- Estimated FCF Growth for the next 10 years: 25%
- Terminal Growth Rate: 3%
- Current FCF: $228.5 million
- Sum of future FCF discounted back to the present: $6,420.4 million
- Current Share Count: 47.515 million
- Intrinsic Value: **$135**
- Margin of Safety: 15%, therefore adjusted Intrinsic Value = $115

Mistakes Made and Lessons Learnt

In this business, if you're good, you're right six times out of 10. You're never going to be right nine times out of 10. — Peter Lynch

As humans, we all make mistakes. Mistakes are part of our evolution, and it can be deemed inevitable. However, what is paramount is not to blame ourselves and put ourselves down. That will get us to nowhere. Instead, we have to ask ourselves why the mistake happened, how can we learn from it and not repeat it in the future. George Bernard Shaw once said, *Success does not consist in never making mistakes but in never making the same one a second time.*

Even the greatest investor in the world, Warren Buffett, had made some glaring mistakes in the past. His biggest mistake and a widely quoted one happened back in 1962 when he started purchasing the textile company called Berkshire Hathaway. It was a struggling New England textile mill when Buffett bought into it and he kept the mill running for 20 years before shutting it down. Buffett said he did not recognize at the point of purchase that the textile business was doomed to continue losing money. He also claimed that buying Berkshire Hathaway had denied him compounded investment returns of about $200 billion, which is twice as much if he had invested those money directly in insurance businesses instead. He quipped, "**When I took control of Berkshire in 1965**, the dumbest thing I could have done was to pursue 'opportunities' to improve and expand the existing textile operation — so for years that's exactly what I did. And then, in a final burst of brilliance, I went out and bought another textile company. Aaaaaaargh! Eventually I came to my senses, heading first into insurance and then into other industries."

In this section, we will discuss some of the mistakes we have made. The reason for this is so that you readers can learn from it and not make the same mistakes as us. Eleanor Roosevelt's quote rings true: *Learn from the mistakes of others. You can't live long enough to make them all yourself.*

Sudhan: I will discuss three of the mistakes below and what I had learnt from them.

First Mistake

I invested in a company called Dapai in end October 2010. Dapai is a Chinese company, listed in Singapore, which is involved in designing, developing, manufacturing and selling of backpacks and luggage under the "Dapai" brand in China. It was the No.1 backpack company in China with a 35.8% market share at the point of purchase. I divested the company just 2 weeks later in early November.

The reasons for divestment are threefold. They are:

(1) Company did a share placement in May 2010 even with lots of cash in hand and negligible debt. It raised money and diluted shareholders' holdings without the need to.
(2) Company has been postponing the opening of 500 new stores, and I was not comfortable with this.
(3) Net profit margins, ROE, ROA have been decreasing throughout the 3 years. Maybe I was blinded by various rosy pictures painted by the company.

Even with all the "negatives" of the company, I went on to invest in the company. I broke a major rule in value investing — "When in doubt, never invest!"

Luckily, I managed to sell off Dapai at a slight profit after deducting commissions. I guess I was plain lazy to research thoroughly and still went on to invest in this company anyway. I was afraid of "missing the boat" as Dapai was "undervalued" at the time of purchase and did not want to miss out on the low price. One of my mentors told me once, "To me, losing opportunity is better than losing money" and that is a tenant to invest by. I would rather lose the opportunity (not getting in at a cheaper price) while researching into Dapai then invest in it and lose money in the end.

In value investing, being disciplined is very critical. I wasn't disciplined enough to research thoroughly. Warren Buffett has said, "The stock market is a no-called-strike game. You don't have to swing at everything — you can wait for your pitch". I learnt from this mistake not to swing at every company that comes my way. It is better to lose opportunity than lose money. Opportunities will be presented every now and then.

Second Mistake

I bought into a China exchange traded fund (ETF) called "United SSE 50 China ETF". It is an ETF listed in Singapore that corresponds to the 50 largest stocks in the SSE 50 index found in the Shanghai Stock Exchange (SSE). I bought into this after many talked about how investing in China will be the next big wave. I bought into the China story, but there were problems like poor corporate governance, high internal debt and inflation. The various problems in China caused the index to drop and so did my ETF. The losses from the SSE 50 ETF dragged my portfolio down immensely. The price could recover in many years' time, but there is an opportunity cost involved. I could put the money in another company that would have been more profitable. Furthermore, the ETF gave no dividends holding on to it was futile. So, I sold it off and lost around 30% of my capital.

The lesson learnt was not to invest in things I did not understand. I did not understand the China story but was bought into it anyway.

Third Mistake

This mistake involves Raffles Medical. I bought into Raffles Medical in June 2009 when I just started off investing. I sold it two months later since the stock price hit the intrinsic value I had calculated. The stock price is now more than double the price I bought at.

I learnt from this episode not to sell a business even if the stock price has reached the intrinsic value. It would have been better to keep the business since the fundamentals were intact and it was still a growing business. From then on, I made a decision that I would only sell if the fundamentals have turned for the worst or if I made a mistake in analysing the business and have to cut loss (like in the Dapai case).

Wei Lin: My biggest mistake thus far is putting too much trust in professionals. As mentioned in the introduction of the book, I gave far too much credit to the professional skillsets of fund managers when I first started. It seemed logical to me that the person who is most in touch with the market would know best. Besides, what can go wrong when the fund manager's decisions were backed by careful analysis of research analysts who graduated with the top honours from some of the best universities in the world?

After reading Peter Lynch's book *One Up on Wall Street* and Professor Burton G. Malkiel's *A Random Walk Down Wall Street*, I had a better understanding of limitations faced by fund managers.

Besides the investment arena, there are also several conflict of interests in the financial planning industry. If you're interested to learn more about such issues, I will highly recommend Tan Kin Lian's book *Practical Guide on Financial Planning* and *Get Value from Your Life Insurance*. He also has a blog which he updates regularly.

So after learning all these, how did I proceed on with my financial expedition? Well simple, I decided to take matters into my own hands. I decided to practise fiscal responsibility and more importantly, I decided that the individual is at times, the best allocator of his own capital as the interests are well aligned.

As for stock selection, my worst decision was Nokia (NOK). My investment thesis for NOK was as such: a business which was quickly losing market share and its innovative advantage over its peers, yet seemed cheap based on valuation.

After a while, it seemed like I was waiting for a straight flush which never came. In fact, matters got worse. Within months after the purchase, NOK's earnings per share went into negative territory. Shareholders were completely devastated. A change of key management personnel was introduced and I had enough. I sold out.

So looking back, where was the mistake? Well, the margin of safety was not perhaps big enough to justify a purchase into a company with lousy business prospects, especially in an industry which was revolutionizing too quickly.

If I may just quote Buffett, "The key to investing is not assessing how much an industry is going to affect society, or how much it will grow, but rather determining the competitive advantage of any given company and, above all, the durability of that advantage. The products or services that have wide, sustainable moats around them are the ones that deliver rewards to investors."

A great company whose business I completely understood yet failed to act upon was Asia Pacific Breweries (APB). It is a fantastic business with an enduring competitive moat. Well, basically, APB sells Tiger Beer and other household beer brands such as Heineken, Anchor and ABC. With a consistent and increasing free cash flow, a strong balance sheet and high Return of Equity of 28.56%, it does not take a rocket scientist to figure out that APB is a fantastic business. The key issue that left me "thumb-sucking" was valuation. I was unwilling to pay, at that point in time, around 25 times earnings for APB, trying hard to haggle by waiting for a market correction that didn't come. On top of that, I was concerned about the low volume of the shares, which affected the bid-ask spread.

Well, turns out, it was an incredibly dumb decision on my part. In less than 6 months after the initial analysis was done, APB shot up to around $50 (from around $30).

Ser Jing: I have been fortunate because I have not made any catastrophic losses in the stock market, *yet*. I have met individuals who started out speculating and lost boatloads of money — some learnt a lesson and started investing, some were scared away for life. For me, my very first proper introduction into the stock market was through Philip Fisher's *Common Stocks and Uncommon Profits*, which gave me a solid grounding in investing, and I have never tried anything besides investing based on fundamentals. But that's not to say I've not made any mistakes. I've made plenty!

Ford is one of the stocks I own in my personal portfolio and it, in fact, has been one of my greatest losers. I purchased it without realizing it had a Credit Arm to its business, which in essence, meant that I was buying a stake in a company that was making and selling cars and making loans. At this stage of my investing life, I am still unable to understand the balance sheet of financial institutions. I made a mistake with Ford because I purchased it without understanding the whole scope of its business and invested in it purely on the back of Motley Fool's recommendation. That is not to say that Motley Fool made a bad recommendation — it was a mistake on my part because Ford was probably not an investment for me. I have since learned not to invest in companies that I do not have a good understanding of.

I will continue to hold Ford because I believe in investing for the long-term, and in doing so, it helps train my temperament because

I only invested in Ford slightly more than 2 years ago, which in my book, is a short-time in investing.

I have also made two-fold mistakes with regard to valuation and timing of purchase. I purchased companies at PEs that were a little too high because I was greedy to have a stake in them and I plowed my desired dollar allocation into them at one shot. I have since learned not to do so. It is ok to purchase great companies at slightly richer valuations provided there is more money on hand to take advantage of further mispricing when prices fall.

Interestingly, I also learnt how I can be easily muddled by The Numbers without consideration for The Story. The cleanest balance sheet coupled with the nicest historical trends in earnings and cash flow would not mean a thing if the company's growth path has been permanently snuffed out. I might have made such a mistake by investing in Dolby Laboratories, which generates a significant amount of its revenues from supplying audio-coding technologies to PC makers. As most of you might have realized, iPads, Macs and generally tablets have been slowly taking over the world and might even supplement PC usage. This would mean that Dolby's room for growth might be permanently stunted. Even though they have started to provide similar audio-coding technologies to mobile devices, it is still insufficient to make up for the PC makers decline. In essence, Dolby's path to growth has been blocked — whether the obstacle is permanent or not, time will tell. It is a potential mistake that I watch very closely.

What I have learnt from this mistake would be to actually think carefully about the potential for quality-growth in sales, earnings and cash-flow of companies that I am invested in and not just invest in them based on the strength of their financial statements.

For what it's worth, financial statements are backward-looking, and even though past performance of a company can often be reliable clues for future performance, it pays to also think about what the company can do to continue their success.

In this journey of investing, expect to make mistakes. The key is not to make mistakes but to learn as much and as quickly as possible. We can reduce our chances of making mistakes by staying within our circle of competence and apply a margin of safety to our intended purchase price.

Important Questions to ponder about…

1. What are some of the mistakes you've made pertaining to investing?
2. Do you discuss them openly and try to learn from them or do you shove it under the carpet?
3. What is the most important lesson you've learnt about investing till date?

Bonus

A bonus issue is an offer of free additional shares to existing shareholders, in direct proportion to their existing shareholding in the company. For example, Keppel Corporation did a bonus issue back in April 2011, which was an offer of 1 for 10. This means that for every 10 shares of Keppel Corporation shares you hold, you will be entitled to 1 free share.

Bonus issues are made out of a company's retained earnings, which are profits built up over the years in the company, after paying out the dividends. The increase in shareholders' equity is offset by a fall in retained earnings. Thus, the company's net worth or equity, as measured by the share capital, remains unchanged. No new funds are raised in a Bonus Issue exercise as well.

Just like in the case of dividends, when the company decides to issue bonus shares, "CB" will be shown beside the company's name, which means "Cum Bonus". When you buy a company on or before CB, you will be entitled to the bonus shares, provided you keep it till "Ex-Bonus" or "XB". If you buy the company on or after XB, you will not be entitled to the bonus shares.

The stock market will adjust the share price proportionately after the bonus issue to account for the increased number of shares in issue and to allow for comparability between prices on the Ex-Date and Cum Dates. The formula to calculate the new share price after the bonus issue is

$$\text{Theoretical Ex-Bonus Price} = (A \times \text{Market Price Per Share})/(A + B)$$

where A = number of shares owned and B = number of bonus issues entitled to.

General Offer

A general offer occurs when an "Offeror" makes a mandatory conditional cash offer (the "Offer") for all the remaining shares of a company that is not owned by the offeror. The company has to be delisted if the free float of the shares (shares held in public hands) of the company falls below 10%, as stipulated in the SGX Listing Manual Rule 723.

An offer provides an opportunity for shareholders to exit from the company at a premium price to the last-traded price of the security. The premium must be high enough to entice shareholders to sell their shares. If shareholders deem the offer price to be undervalued, the offeror might not have enough acceptance to delist the company.

For example, in October 2010, Thomson Medical Centre was delisted at S$1.75/share, which was a premium of 62% to the last-traded price, prior to the offer announcement. The offer price of S $1.75/share, which carried a P/E of 32.3, was more than enough to entice most of the shareholders. The P/E of another medical company, Raffles Medical Group, had a P/E of only around 21. A more recent example of an offer would be that of Asia Pacific Breweries, which was bought over by Heineken.

Important Questions to ponder about…

1. What are some of the corporate actions in SGX?
2. Is it wise or unwise to subscribe to a rights issue done by your company?
3. What do you think is the downside of a general offer made to a company you own?

Conclusion

Thank you so, so, so much for reading till the end. We have tried our best to pen down our thoughts and experiences for the benefit of you. We have nothing more to add, except for a few parting words.

We hope that the knowledge you glean from this book will not restrict you to just the local markets. Fundamentals-based investing works across the globe, though there are definitely differences to consider. Please do not feel pigeon-holed by geography alone — the world is your oyster!

Investing is a never-ending learning process. We are learning something new about it every day, and we hope you do, too.

Okay, as Munger likes to say, this time we really "have nothing more to add". We wish you, Happy Investing.

Cheers,

Sudhan, Ser Jing and Wei Lin

Appendix: Financial Statements

Income Statement

Let us take a look at the Income Statement of XYZ Corporation, a business that owns a chain of coffee shops where they sell cups of coffee, other beverages and food items to customers. The Income Statement measures the profit of a business over a certain period of time, usually for three months, half a year and one full year. The numbers presented in the Income Statement are cumulative; it means the Income Statement for the first three months is added to the income statement for the next three months and so on to arrive at the Income Statement for the full financial year. In the Income Statement, you will notice a number of items on the left, starting with Sales Revenue. These line items are all crucial in determining a figure that is so scrutinised by the financial press — Earnings Per Share. Now, let us see what these line items actually mean.

- Sales Revenue is the total amount of money brought in by selling goods or services to customers. In 2008, XYZ Corporation managed to sell $10 million worth of coffee, beverages and food to customers.
- Cost of Sales is the cost of raw materials needed to produce the good or service that is being sold to customers. In the case of XYZ Corporation, raw materials for its coffee shop business would consist of coffee powder, sugar, condensed milk, raw food ingredients, etc. In 2008, the cost of these raw ingredients amounted to $5 million.

- Gross Profit is the profit that is left over after deducting Cost of Sales from Sales Revenue. XYZ Corporation had Gross Profit of $5 million in 2008.

  Gross Profit = Sales Revenue – Cost of Sales

- Selling, General and Admin Expense (SG&A) consists of worker's salaries, rents to be paid, marketing and advertising costs, research and development costs etc. XYZ Corporation, which operates coffee shops, would have the bulk of this expense in the form of worker's salary, rents and marketing and advertising costs. In 2008, they amounted to $2.5 million.
- Depreciation and Amortisation (D&A) is a unique expense that is different from Cost of Sales and SG&A in the sense that no real money has been used up in the case of D&A. If no money has been used up, why is it an expense? The reason is because there are certain equipment and properties that can be re-used over and over again in the course of selling goods or services to customers. Some classic examples include computers, office furniture, manufacturing equipment, delivery vehicles, manufacturing plants, etc. These items incur a one-time payment when they are purchased for use but are used repeatedly over many months or even years. Such items are thus classified as an Asset and the cost of purchase for them is recorded in the Balance Sheet.

  As these items are being used, natural wear-and-tear occurs such that the items eventually break down and have to be replaced. Depreciation is thus an estimation of this wear-and-tear process in monetary terms. The corresponding Asset on the Balance Sheet is then decreased by the same amount as the Depreciation expense. Amortisation works in essentially the same way as Depreciation, except the Amortisation expense is meant for the Intangible Assets and Goodwill account in the Balance Sheet. We will cover more on this later, so do not worry if the idea still seems fuzzy to you.

For now, just remember that D&A is an expense, but is different from Cost of Goods Sold and SG&A. For XYZ Corporation's case, equipment that would be needed to run a coffee shop might include tables, chairs, utensils, coffee press, stoves, the physical coffee shops itself, etc. The D&A expense of $1.2 million in 2008 estimates the amount of wear-and-tear that this equipment went through in the process of making and selling coffee, beverages and food to customers to reduce the PP&E account in the Balance Sheet by the corresponding amount and did not affect the Intangible Assets and Goodwill account.

- Operating Earnings is the profit that is left over after deducting SG&A and D&A from Gross Profit. Operating Earnings for XYZ Corporation in 2008 was $1.3 million.

  Operating Earnings = Gross Profit – SG&A – D&A

- Interest Expense is the interest that is paid for any debt that XYZ Corporation owes to other parties. In the course of doing business, some companies might need more money and thus they can either look for investors or borrow money from other parties. When money is borrowed, the lender would require a certain interest rate to be paid on the debt each year, much like how an individual has to pay interest to the banks for a housing loan. XYZ Corporation had zero interest expense in 2008 because it does not owe any money (we can check this from XYZ Corporation's balance sheet — more on that later).
- Income Tax Expense is the tax that a business has to pay to its government on the profit that it makes after deducting Interest Expense from Operating Earnings. It is very similar in concept as to how you have to pay income tax to IRAS (for the case of people working in Singapore) in April every year based on your income for the previous year. For XYZ Corporation, it was subjected to an income tax rate of 30% in 2008 and had to pay $390,000 in Income Tax.

Income Tax Expense = Income Tax Rate × (Operating Earnings – Interest Expense)

- Net Income is the profit that a business has made after deducting all expenses. In 2008, XYZ Corporation made $2.1 million in profit from selling $10 million worth of coffee in their coffee shops.

  Net Income = Operating Earnings – Income Tax Expense

Okay, now we have just two more line items to go before we conclude the Income Statement. Hang in there!

- Average No. of Diluted Shares Outstanding is the total number of shares that the company is made up of, inclusive of all options, warrants, or convertible debts that might be converted into shares. Options, warrants and convertible debts are financial instruments issued by a business that give their holders the right to exchange these instruments into shares at a previously agreed upon price. Should these instruments be converted into shares, existing shareholders' stake in a business would become smaller — hence the word "Diluted". In XYZ Corporation's case in 2008, each existing and potential share is entitled to 1/10,000 of the Net Income, Assets, and Liabilities, etc. of the business. It is important to use the Average No. of Diluted Shares Outstanding figure instead of the Average No. of Shares Outstanding because you would want to see how much of the business you actually own if the option, warrant and convertible debt holders were to convert these financial instruments into shares — in extreme cases, the difference between the diluted and un-diluted figures can be massive and that is a dangerous situation for existing shareholders because their stake in the business can suddenly shrink.
- Earnings Per Share (EPS) is as its name suggests, the profit that each share of the business is entitled to. XYZ Corporation had EPS of $0.091 in 2008.

  EPS = Net Income/Average No. of Diluted Shares Outstanding

Congratulations! You have made it through the Income Statement and finally got a glimpse on how a business arrives at this EPS figure which is very widely used in the financial media. In the "Valuation" section, EPS would be used often, so please keep the formula for EPS in mind as we progress through "The Numbers" section. Note that the Income Statement only gives us the profit or loss that a business makes but not the financial condition of the business. You might know Larry's monthly income from his pay-slip, but you would be unable to tell if he has huge outstanding bank loans or whether his bank account is flush with cash. For a business, the situation is similar — the Income Statement is analogous to Larry's payslip, while the Balance Sheet would be similar to a record of Larry's loans and bank account. So, let us now move on to the Balance Sheet — a measure of the financial condition of the business.

Balance Sheet

In the Balance Sheet, the most important formula to remember would be

Total Assets = Total Liabilities + Total Shareholders Equity

The Balance Sheet records the Assets, Liabilities and Equity of a business. The Balance Sheet does not show the flow of activities in the business's Assets, Liabilities and Equity accounts and when a Balance Sheet is prepared, it is as though the financial condition of the business is frozen in time for a split second (John Tracy). Let us run through each account on the Balance Sheet of XYZ Corporation to help you understand what they mean.

- Current Assets are Assets that are held for sale to customers and that can be converted into cash within one year.

Current Assets = Cash & Equivalents + Accounts Receivable + Inventory + Prepaid Expenses

- Cash & Equivalents consist of cold-hard cash found in the business's bank account, as well as financial investments such as stocks, short-and-long term government bonds, corporate bonds, etc. They are liquid investments that can be converted into cash at short notice. The Cash and Equivalents account is tallied in the Cash Flow statement (more on that later). For XYZ Corporation's case, in 2008, they had $3 million in Cash and Equivalents, of which the breakdown between "Cash" and "Equivalents" was not given.
- Account Receivables are sales that have been made to customers but in which the cash has not actually been transferred to the company yet at the time the Balance Sheet was being prepared. Out of the $10 million in Sales Revenue that XYZ Corporation booked in 2008, $2.5 million has yet to be received by the company and that is reflected in its Account Receivables line. Reasons for such discrepancies between selling the good/service and receiving the cash could be due to the extension of credit to customers, such as invoicing all orders only at the end of every month.
- Inventory consists of the cost of making goods for sale/services to customers that will be sold later. They are usually broken down into three categories: (1) Raw Materials, (2) Goods-in-Progress, and (3) Finished Products. For example, coffee powder, unsold-canned beverages and raw food items that are stored in the coffee shops are considered as Inventory items for XYZ Corporation. In 2008, Inventory was $1 million for XYZ Corporation.
- Prepaid Expenses are operating expenses that have already been paid in full before the good/service has been consumed and thus, are recorded as an Asset on the Balance Sheet. Insurance premiums are a good example of prepaid expenses (John Tracy). For example, XYZ Corporation might have paid insurance premiums for one years' worth of coverage for fire accidents in their coffee shops. The premiums have been paid up-front, but the coverage extends for a year (the insurance policy is slowly being "consumed" as the year

progresses). XYZ Corporation had $500,000 in pre-paid expenses in 2008.

- Non-current Assets are long-term operating assets required for the business's operations and would normally not be converted into cash in one year.

Non-current Assets = Property, Plant and Equipment + Intangible Assets and Goodwill

- Property, Plant, and Equipment (PP&E) as its name suggests, consists of the office buildings, factories, factory equipment, etc. that a business requires to conduct its daily operations. For a coffee shop business like XYZ Corporation, PP&E will include items such as tables, chairs, utensils, coffee-press, stoves, and the physical coffee shops itself, etc. as mentioned earlier. You might also recall the lengthy discussion of D&A which involves the PP&E and Intangible Assets and Goodwill account in the Balance Sheet. When an equipment or property is purchased for business and is required for long-term operations, the purchase price is classified as an Asset under the PP&E account on the Balance Sheet. However, this equipment and property will eventually have to be replaced and the Depreciation expense is used to capture their "decline". The PP&E account will have to be reduced by the same amount as the Depreciation expense. At the same time however, more investments can be made under the PP&E account and these investments are captured under the Cash Flow Statement in the Purchase of Property, Plant and Equipment line in which case, PP&E will have to be increased by the same amount as the investments made. In all, the PP&E account in the Balance Sheet has to change in the same amount as the net difference between Purchase of Property, Plant, and Equipment and Depreciation.

  If you have ever purchased a car, you will know that keeping all other things constant, a car that is five years old will be worth less than one that is two years old. The difference in price is due to the concept of Depreciation. You will notice that no cash was being paid by you even though your car is worth less at the fifth year as compared to the second year of ownership. That is why Depreciation (and Amortisation) is a different kind of expense as compared to SG&A and Cost of Sales. The latter two expenses involve a transaction of real cash from XYZ Corporation to their suppliers, but D&A does not involve any cash outlay even though it is considered an expense on the Income Statement. In 2008, XYZ Corporation had $10 million worth of PP&E and you can see how its PP&E account has increased by $100,000 in 2009 because of the Depreciation expense of $1.1 million and Purchase of Property, plant and Equipment cash outflow of $1.2 million in 2009 resulting in a net increase of $100,000 for the PP&E account in the 2009 Balance Sheet.

- Intangible Assets and Goodwill are assets that do not have a physical presence or form. Good examples of Intangible Assets are intellectual properties and brand names. Goodwill arises from the difference between the purchase price and book value (an accounting term which will be explained later) of a company that is being acquired. The Intangible Assets and Goodwill account will change by the net difference between the Amortisation expense on the Income Statement and the Purchase of Intangible Assets line on the Cash Flow Statement. Amortisation occurs when the business feels that the Intangible Assets it has is no longer able to produce the same earnings power as before and so, would reduce the asset at management's own discretion under the Amortisation expense. XYZ Corporation had $5 million worth of Intangible Assets and Goodwill and it remained constant in 2009 because the Purchase of Intangible Assets cash outflow was zero while no Amortisation occurred.

- Current Liabilities are claims on Assets that would depend on the conversion of Current Assets into cash for their payment (John Tracy) within the year.

  Current Liabilities = Accounts Payable + Accrued Expenses Payable + Income Tax Payable + Short-Term Debt and Current Portion of Long-Term Debt

- Accounts Payable is a Liability that occurs naturally for almost every type of business. It arises from buying on credit. For example, the coffee powder and raw food ingredients that XYZ Corporation requires would likely be paid a few weeks *after* delivery of the physical goods itself, thus creating an Accounts Payable of $1.1 million for XYZ Corporation in 2008.
- Accrued Expenses Payable are unpaid expenses that build up over time. Examples of such expenses can include utility bills that have been incurred but not billed to the company yet or accumulated vacation and sick leave pay that is owed to employees (John Tracy). XYZ Corporation had Accrued Expenses Payable of $300,00 in 2008.
- Income Tax Payable is the portion of Income Tax Expenses that is still unpaid at the time when the Balance Sheet is being prepared. XYZ Corporation still owed the tax authorities $200,000 out of the $390,000 Income Tax Expenses that it had to pay.
- Short-Term Debt and Current Portion of Long-Term Debt consists of bonds, bank loans or other debt instruments that are due to be repaid within a year. XYZ Corporation had $0 in this particular account in 2008 — a sign of a conservatively financed company.
- Non-current Liabilities are claims on Assets that have to be repaid after more than one year. In XYZ Corporation's example, the only component of Non-current Liabilities consists of Long-Term Debt.
- Long-Term Debt consists of bonds, bank loans or other debt instruments that are due to be repaid after more than one

year — different debts can have different maturity dates. We can see that XYZ Corporation is a very conservatively financed company because it does not have any debt whatsoever and that is generally a very good sign for most companies.

- Equity, also known as Book Value is the source of ownership capital in the business and it is what the owners of the business, i.e., shareholders, will *theoretically* be able to claim after selling all of what the business owns (Assets) to pay off all of what it owes (Liabilities).

Total Shareholders Equity = Total Assets – Total Liabilities

or

Total Shareholders Equity = Share Capital + Retained Earnings

- Share Capital is the initial capital that shareholders paid for a stake in the business when it first issued shares. In XYZ Corporation's case in 2008, shareholders paid a total of $10 million for the 10 million shares that were initially issued by the company. That works out to be $1 per share.
- Retained Earnings are the portion of Net Income that is retained within the business after dividend distributions to shareholders for growth or to maintain its current operations. XYZ Corporation had $10.4 million worth of Retained Earnings in 2008.

We want to congratulate you again for making it through the Balance Sheet section as you move along your quest to understand The Numbers. There might seem to be plenty of accounts within the Balance Sheet to look at but fret not, as we will discuss what are the truly important numbers to take note of when we *analyse* financial statements to look for investment opportunities in different businesses. All right, so we only have one more financial statement to go — the Cash Flow Statement. Are you ready? 'Cause we certainly are!

Cash Flow Statement

We have finally come to the Cash Flow Statement to round up the trio of Financial Statements that any publicly listed business has to prepare. Even though the financial media often focuses their attention onto the Income Statement, the Cash Flow Statement is arguably more important. Why? It's because the Cash Flow statement records the *actual* cash that is flowing into and out of the business. Net Income might not always reflect the actual cash-flow situation of a business as a business can always record Revenues but not collect them till two years later (just an exaggerated example!). In fact, the Cash Flow Statement is so important that we always strive to find businesses that are producing ample Cash Flow From Operating Activities (CFO). If a business shows great Net Income, but a very spotty CFO, then it is a red flag that something weird with the business *might* be going on and any would-be investors should scrutinise the situation carefully. Over time, the CFO should move roughly in tandem with the changes in Revenue, otherwise, something is really wrong!

The Cash Flow Statement is also cumulative, like the Income Statement. This means that if we want to know the Cash Flow situation for the whole of 2012, we can prepare a Cash Flow statement for each day in 2012 and add them all up. Of course, we don't really look at 365 Cash Flow Statements per year. Most businesses prepare the Cash Flow Statement every three months, just like the Income Statement and Balance Sheet.

The Cash Flow Statement is further broken into three parts: (1) Cash Flow From Operating Activities (CFO), (2) Cash Flow From Investing Activities (CFI), and (3) Cash Flow From Financing Activities (CFF).

CFO, as its name suggests, records the actual cash flowing into and out of the business from its daily operations. Activities such as buying inventory, selling a cup of coffee, paying bills for cooking-gas, etc. all form part of the cash inflow and outflow stemming from its normal day-to-day business activities and is captured under CFO.

CFI records the cash that is used by the business when it is investing in itself. For example, if XYZ Corporation bought a small property to open a new coffee shop, that would be money that is spent on re-investment into the business and would be captured in CFI. There are also times when the business would sell some of these investments; maybe XYZ Corporation has closed down one shop and wants to sell the now-empty shop house. The cash from the sale would be recorded under investing activities as well because the sold item (or property, in this case) is not part of the business's normal operations. But in XYZ Corporation's case, we know there's no sale of any long-term investment-related items because "Sale of Property, Plant, and Equipment" does not appear in the CFI section.

CFF records the cash flows from the business to its owners and creditors. We shall next proceed with the individual line items in the Cash Flow Statement.

- The first line item in a Cash Flow Statement is Net Income, which is obtained from the Income Statement.
- Decrease (Increase) in Accounts Receivable, is as the name suggests, the change in the Accounts Receivable item in the Balance Sheet from one year to the next. For example, the Decrease (Increase) in Accounts Receivable for 2009 measures the change in the Accounts Receivable line in the Balance Sheet between 2008 and 2009. Due to our naming convention, a decrease in Accounts Receivable in 2009 compared to 2008 will be given a positive number, similarly, an increase will be given a negative number. What we need to know is that any decrease in Accounts Receivable will *add* to cash flows and any increase will *subtract* from cash flows. We can see that in 2009, Decrease (Increase) in Accounts Receivable took away $600,000 from cash flows.
- Decrease (Increase) in Inventory and Decrease (Increase) in Prepaid Expenses is similar in concept to Accounts Receivable with the only

difference being that it is measuring the change in Inventory and Prepaid Expenses respectively on the Balance Sheet.

- Increase (Decrease) in Accounts Payable tracks the changes in the Accounts Payable line item on the balance sheet for the time period that the Cash Flow statement is being prepared for. As an example, Accounts Payable *decreased* by $50,000 from 2008 to 2009. This change is reflected in the Cash Flow Statement under the Increase (Decrease) in Accounts Payable line. If Accounts Payable increased on the Balance Sheet, this means that the company has spent a lesser amount of cash to pay his suppliers for that reporting period. It is usually a good thing to see because that means the company you are investigating has clout amongst its suppliers and can afford to dictate payment terms.
- Similarly, Accrued Expenses and Income Taxes are treated the same as Accounts Payable in the Cash Flow Statement.
- As mentioned earlier, Depreciation and Amortisation expenses in the Income Statement do not reflect any real changes in Cash Flow and so, any Depreciation and Amortisation expenses will have to be added to Net Income to get a true reflection of how cash is flowing into-and-out of the business.
- Cash Flow from Operating Activities, or CFO, is arrived at by adding the following items to Net Income; Decrease (Increase) in Accounts Receivable; Decrease (Increase) in Inventory; Decrease (Increase) in Prepaid Expenses; Increase (Decrease) in Accounts Payable; Increase (Decrease) in Accrued Expenses Payable; Increase (Decrease) in Income Tax Payable; Depreciation and Amortisation.
- Purchase of Property, Plant and Equipment (PP&E) is also known as Capital Expenditures or CapEx. PP&E tracks the real cash outlay a company makes in long-term re-investments of physical objects into its own business either for growth or to maintain the business's current operations. For example, XYZ Corporation's coffee presses and cooking equipment might be outdated and so, the management

of the company has decided to spend $1.2 million to purchase new equipment for its existing coffee shops in 2009.

- Purchase of Intangible Assets and Goodwill involves cash outlays to purchase assets that have no physical presence but yet surely exist. Trademarks and corporate logos are great examples of intangible assets. We wouldn't know the exact price of Coca-Cola's cursive words or Nike's famous "swoosh", but we definitely know it would cost anyone a bomb if they wanted to purchase or rent the logos for any commercial purpose. We can see that XYZ Corporation did not purchase any intangible assets or goodwill in 2009.
- Cash Flow From Financing Activities is simply the summation of; Purchase of Property, Plant, and Equipment; and Purchase of Intangible Assets.
- Proceeds from Short-Term Debt are the inflows of cash coming from short-term loans taken up by a business. In Financial Statements, "short-term debt" refers to any debt instrument that must be repaid within one year. As an aside, the most common debt instruments are bank loans and bonds — there are more colourful forms of corporate debt, but we shall not go into them. How this works is, imagine a company that has just took up a bank loan on January 2013 that will be due on December 2013 for $1 million. This $1 million will be reflected on the Proceeds from Short-Term Debt line item in the Cash Flow item. In XYZ Corporation's case, they did not take on any short-term debt from 2008 to 2009.
- Proceeds from Long-Term Debt mean the exact same thing as Proceeds from Short-Term Debt, with the only difference being the debt that is being assumed is of a long-term nature. And, long-term here refers to any debt instruments that will mature and be required to be paid up in more than a year. XYZ Corporation did not take in any long-term debt from 2008 to 2009.
- Cash Dividends Paid measures the actual cash that is paid out by the company to shareholders over the course of the reporting

period. Companies often announce a dividend payment of $X per share at the end of their financial calendar. This payment will only commence after shareholder approval (usually, it is approved because, who doesn't like regular pay checks?) during the Annual General Meeting. However, the shareholder approvals would have taken place after the reporting period of the Financial Year and so, there will come situations where an already declared-dividend has not been paid out and will only be reflected in the Cash Flow Statement at some later reporting period. In any case, the Cash Dividends Paid will still be a very close proxy for the actual dividend-situation of a company. We can see that XYZ Corporation paid out $300,000 in cash dividends in 2009.

- Issuance of Stock tracks the cash a company receives from giving out stock to either new or existing shareholders. Rights Issues are familiar events with shareholders in the local stock market and would be covered later but suffice it to say that, whatever proceeds coming in from a Rights Issue would be recorded in this particular line item in the Cash Flow Statement. XYZ Corporation did not issue any new stock in 2008 to 2012, judging by the zero-figure in the Cash Flow Statement for Issuance of Stock.
- Total Increase (Decrease) in Cash is simply the summation of; Cash Flow From Operating Activities; Cash Flow From Investing Activities; and Cash Flow From Financing Activities.
- Cash Balance at Start of the Year is the Cash & Equivalents line item in the Balance Sheet for the previous year from the current reporting period. For example, in 2008, XYZ Corporation had $3 million in the Cash & Equivalents line item in the Balance Sheet and this was reflected in the Cash Balance at Start of the Year line item for 2009 in the Cash Flow Statement.
- Cash Balance at End of the Year is the summation of; Total Increase (Decrease) in Cash; and Cash Balance at Start of the Year. Astute readers will notice that the Cash Balance at End of the Year line item on the Cash Flow Statement will reflect the same figure

as the Cash & Equivalents line item on the Balance Sheet for the same reporting period. So, for 2009, XYZ Corporation had $4.06 million for both Cash Balance at the End of the Year and Cash & Equivalents.

Finally, we're done with the explanation of each of the line items in a rudimentary Financial Statement — give yourself a pat on the back! It can get a tad confusing learning all these accounting-lingo, but trust us, businesses suddenly make a lot more sense after knowing what these figures mean. Most investing or accounting books will talk about these three statements as though they are independent entities. *But*, it is not the case — the three Financial Statements are *inter-linked*. One statement drives the other and they do not exist independently.

We would now like to go one step further by high-lighting to you, how the Income Statement, Balance Sheet and Cash Flow Statement are related to each other.

How Are They All Linked Together

We've decided to showcase how these numbers interact with each other briefly and the idea comes from the brilliant accounting book, *How to Read a Financial Report* by John Tracy. We'll start with the Income Statement and how each line of the Income Statement is linked to the Balance Sheet. Then, we'll look at how each line in the Balance Sheet is linked to the Cash Flow statement.

Starting with the Income Statement and Balance Sheet

- Sales Revenue is linked to Accounts Receivable. Sales that have been booked but which cash has not been received during the reporting period generally shows up as Accounts Receivable.
- Cost of Sales is linked to Inventory. We know that Inventory is valued at the cost of producing a product or service. So, any Inventory on

the Balance Sheet at the end of the reporting period will be charged to the Cost of Sales expense as the inventory is cleared in the next reporting period.

- Selling, General & Admin Expense is linked to three different accounts on the Balance Sheet, namely; Prepaid Expenses; Accounts Payable; and Accrued Expenses Payable. The Selling, General & Admin Expense are a form of Operating Expense and these are expenses that occur whenever a business conducts its daily affairs. What happens is, as these daily expenses are being incurred, some of them will be for services or items that have already been paid for but will only be delivered at a later period. These would fall under Prepaid Expenses.

  Selling, General & Admin Expenses will also include services or items that have already been consumed but which have not been paid for and these will go into the Accounts Payable and/or Accrued Expenses Payable accounts on the Balance Sheet.
- Depreciation and Amortisation is linked to the Property, Plant and Equipment and Intangible Assets and Goodwill accounts on the Balance Sheet. Specifically, Depreciation is linked to PP&E, while Amortisation is linked to Intangibles and Goodwill. For the reporting period, PP&E will decrease by the amount that is indicated by the Depreciation expense on the Income Statement. The same goes for Intangible Assets and Goodwill with Amortisation.
- Interest Expense is linked to Short-Term Debt and Long-Term Debt on the Balance Sheet. The debts carried by any company will have interest payments for the reporting period and it is reflected by the Interest Expense line on the Income Statement. The Interest Expense is also linked to Accrued Expense Payable as the interest payments on the debts might have been incurred but not paid out yet.
- Income Tax Expense is linked to the Income Tax Payable account on the Balance Sheet. The rational is the same as how Interest

Expense is linked to Accrued Expense Payable — there might be income taxes that have already been marked as 'paid' but the actual cash might not have been paid out yet.

- Net Income is linked to the Retained Earnings account on the Balance Sheet. We can obtain the Retained Earnings account by subtracting Cash Dividends Paid (from the Cash Flow Statement) from Net Income.

Now, for the Balance Sheet and Cash Flow Statement

The links between the Balance Sheet and the Cash Flow Statement have already been described previously when we went through each line item on the Cash Flow Statement. So now, we hope you have a better idea of what Financial Statements are, what do they mean and how they are inter-locked with one another. With the basic (and we stress the word, *basic*, here) accounting back-ground knowledge, let us move on how to make sense of these numbers when we try to make investing decisions.

The Real Numbers to Look At For Investment Decisions

Well done! You have worked hard to slog through the Income Statement, Balance Sheet and Cash Flow Statement sections to gain an understanding of how to read them. We would now like to discuss the really important numbers within the financial statements, some trends within those numbers and financial ratios that can help us to make quick and dirty decisions on the attractiveness of a business for our investment dollars. As always, we would again return to XYZ Corporation's financial statements for use as examples. Bear in mind however, that these important numbers/trends/ratios cannot be used in isolation and they must be *analysed together* to come up with a coherent picture of the business and financial conditions of the company.

Checks for Profitability

1. **Has Sales Revenue been increasing throughout the years?**
   It is a positive sign if Sales Revenue has been increasing throughout the years. The most powerful way for a business to grow would be to sell more of its goods or services to customers and rising Sales Revenue would reflect that positive trend. It is also very useful to observe how Sales Revenue changes during economic recessions as it can give us strong clues on the resiliency of a company's business model and can tell us if a business exhibits strong cyclicality. Of course, if the last economic recession happened more than 20 years ago, the business might have changed so much that no useful information can be extracted from that set of old data and so, if we want to study the effects of recession on a business, it would only be logical to study it if the latest recession happened fairly recently. We can see that Sales Revenue for XYZ Corporation has been steadily rising from $10 million in 2008 to $20.485 million in 2012, at a time when the global economy was in shambles due to the financial crisis in the USA in 2007–2009. This shows how powerful XYZ Corporation's business model is.

2. **Has Net Income been positive and increasing throughout the years?**
   Even though rising revenue is generally a good thing for a business, we do not want to see a business losing money even though it is selling more goods and services to customers. After all, according to Joel Greenblatt (The Little Book that Still Beats the Market), the best way to raise sales would be to sell a dollar note for 50 cents! We would also want to observe how Net Income changes during economic recessions for much the same reasons as it is with Sales Revenue, in addition to checking how the cost structure of a business might be affected. Our favourite coffee shop shows a very favourable trend as its Net Income has increased from $910,000 in 2008 to $4.484 million in 2012 — a stellar achievement!

3. **Has EPS been positive and increasing throughout the years?** The difference between Net Income and EPS is subtle, yet important. Recall that EPS is the profit that each share of the business is entitled to. If a company issues more and more shares to new shareholders throughout the years, our existing stake in the business will decrease — thus there might be a situation where Net Income is increasing but EPS remains flat or even decreasing due to massive dilution. However, we also do not want a situation where EPS is increasing but Sales Revenue and Net Income has been staying flat. EPS can increase if the latter two numbers are stagnant due to management buying back shares, which causes our existing stake in the business to increase. If the EPS increase is solely due to buying back of shares, there are only that many shares that management can buy-back before they need the cash for other needs within the business. Thus, the best way for EPS to increase is to have rising Sales Revenue and Net Income. We can see that XYZ Corporation has managed its business well to increase its EPS from \$0.091 in 2008 to \$0.448 in 2012.

4. **Has Gross Margin Trends improved throughout the years?** The formula for Gross Margin is given below. It is an important ratio to track because it shows the pricing power of a business in relation to the cost of its raw materials (Pat Dorsey). If the Gross Margins of a business has been steadily decreasing throughout the years, it would signal a loss in pricing power and this trend is something that we do not want to see in our investments. The obvious best case scenario would be to see rising Gross Margin trends. However, Gross Margins that remain steady within a narrow range would not be a bad thing too (the natural business cycles and unpredictability of life in general would dictate that the numbers we see in Financial Statements cannot move with clockwork-like precision). Bear in mind, however, that it is the trend, and not the absolute number that is important here. This is because companies in different industries have very different cost structures and so a

Gross Margin of 30% might be excellent for a retail business (e.g., Walmart), but extremely poor for a licensing business (e.g., Dolby). XYZ Corporation saw its Gross Margins increase from 50% in 2008 to a relatively narrow band of 54–57% in 2009–2012. That is of course, a great thing to see in a business.

Gross Margin = Gross Profit/Sales Revenue

5. **Has Operating Margin Trends improved throughout the years?**
Operating Margins measure the income that is derived from a business's normal operations relative to its Sales Revenue. We want to look at the trend for Operating Margins as well because we want to see how changes in Sales Revenue can affect the overall profitability of a company. For Sales Revenue to grow, more often than not, more employees and equipment etc. are needed. The trick for management is to ensure that Sales Revenue grows at a faster proportion than the growth in the relevant expenses. This difference in Sales Revenue growth rate and expenses can be shown in Operating Margin trends. A deteriorating trend is a no-no, an improving one, a big yes! Imagine a situation where Gross Margins remain steady while Operating Margins are improving — this shows that each dollar of new expense that is required for growth in the business is generating more than a dollar in Sales Revenue growth and that is a great situation we want to see in our potential investments!

This does feel a little like detective sleuthing, doesn't it? Like Sudhan said, it can be fun being a capitalist Sherlock Holmes! Now, take note that, there is no absolute number that is important here, similar to Gross Margins, and it is the trend that we, as investors, want to take note of. XYZ Corporation actually saw its Operating Margin increase from 13% in 2008 to 31.3% in 2012, a fantastic achievement.

Operating Margin = Operating Earnings/Sales Revenue

6. **Have Net Margin Trends improved throughout the years?**
   Net Margins measure the profitability of a business's operations *after* taking into account debt payments and corporate income taxes. Now, why are Net Margin trends important if we are already looking at Operating Margins? The reason for doing so is because we want to see if the growth in the company's Sales Revenue was achieved due to taking on excess Debt in which case, the interest payments on both Short and Long-Term Debt might eat up any Operating Earnings, leading to smaller Net Income or even negative Net Income in the worst case scenario. Since we already knew that XYZ Corporation does not carry any debt on its Balance Sheet, it should come as no surprise to see that the business saw its Net Margins increase from 9.1% in 2008 to 21.9%. As with the general rule for Gross Margins and Operating Margins, there are no absolute numbers for Net Margins that a business has to display for it to be considered a prudent investment choice — different industries have different characteristics.

   Net Margins = Net Income/Sales Revenue

7. **Has Return on Equity held steady or increased over the years?**
   Return on Equity is one of Warren Buffett's favourite measures of overall profitability of a business, provided the business does not carry an unusually large amount of debt or liabilities on its Balance Sheet. It measures the profits per dollar of shareholder's capital (Pat Dorsey) and a declining Return on Equity might signal deteriorating economic characteristics for the business in question. Different industries or businesses at different growth-stages would exhibit different figures for Returns on Equity that are deemed good. We would ideally like to own businesses with Returns on Equity of above 12% as a *general* benchmark provided there is relatively little Total Debt on its Balance Sheet.

   Return on Equity = Net Income/Total Shareholders Equity

Checks for Financial Stability

We have already gone through seven important figures and ratios that give us a good picture of a business's profitability. Now, we would like to look at the important figures on the Balance Sheet that can give us a clear picture on the financial stability of the business, i.e., will it run into any financial difficulties soon or worse, be in danger of bankruptcy?

1. **Does the Business carry more Cash & Equivalents than Debt?**
   The most *conservative* check for the financial health of a business would be to see if it has more Cash & Equivalents as compared to Total Debt on its Balance Sheet. As Buffett says, *I do not like debt and do not like to invest in companies that have too much debt, particularly long-term debt. With long-term debt, increases in interest rates can drastically affect company profits and make future cash flows less predictable.* With more Cash & Equivalents, there is no chance of the business going bankrupt and even if it has to pay off any of its debt at the shortest of notices, it would not have to sell off any profit-making Assets at fire-sale prices to meet debt payments because the Cash on hand is more than enough to cover the Debt obligations. Ser Jing particularly likes to see the businesses he invests in carry more Cash than Debt. Even though this criteria is certainly the most *conservative*, it might not be the *best* because there are other profitable businesses that have more debt than cash but if this criteria allows you to pass the *sleep-at-night* test, then we say "Choose it!"

   Total Debt = Short-Term Debt and Current Portion of Long-Term Debt + Long-Term Debt

2. **Is the Current Ratio and Quick Ratio of the business positive?**
   The Current Ratio gives us a good idea of the liquidity of the business — i.e, how easily can a business pay off its Current Liabilities. It measures the short-term liquidity of a business and

as a *very rough guide*, a Current Ratio of 1.5 should mean that the business has more than adequate liquidity to meet its normal operating needs. The Quick Ratio is an even more conservative measure of the short-term liquidity of the business by removing Inventory from Current Assets. The reason for doing so is that Inventory can sometimes be worth less than the value ascribed to in on the Balance Sheet (Pat Dorsey). Again, as a *very rough guide*, a Quick Ratio more than 1 would be an excellent figure.

Current Ratio = Current Assets/Current Liabilities

Quick Ratio = (Current Assets – Inventory)/Current Liabilities

3. **Is the Debt to Equity Ratio of the business below 1?**
   Debt to Equity is a more general look at a company's financial health. The *general rule of thumb* is that the lower the number, the better. It is of course, a less conservative measure of financial health of a business as compared to Point 1. under **Checks for Financial Stability**.

   Debt to Equity Ratio = Total Debt/Total Shareholders Equity

Checks for Cash Flow Quality and Dividend Payouts

1. **Has Operating Cash Flow been positive and increasing throughout the years?**
   The Income Statement is easily manipulated by management, as almost every single item on the income statement involves estimates by management. As a result, a business that posts great figures for Net Income might not actually see real cash coming in at all. The real cash that is flowing into the business from its daily operations is reflected in its Operating Cash Flow. Thus, we would ideally want to see a general trend of Operating Cash Flow increasing as Revenue increases, in roughly the same percentage terms. Businesses that are Net Income positive but yet have negative Operating Cash Flow

might be playing accounting games and as a prudent investor, there are much better investment choices out there than to be involved with a potential stink-bomb.

2. **Has Free Cash Flow been positive and increasing throughout the years?**
   Free Cash Flow is the residual cash from Operating Cash Flow that is left-over after the company has invested in assets that it requires to maintain its business (also known as Capital Expenditures). Free Cash Flow can be used for acquisitions for growth, repurchasing of shares and to pay out dividends to shareholders without resorting to borrowing money or issuing more shares for capital. Businesses that can produce great Free Cash Flow, in addition to Operating Cash Flow are generally businesses that can produce great returns for shareholders as the cash can be returned to shareholders in terms of dividends or retained within the business to grow further. As mentioned in The Story, the presence of significant Free Cash Flow is a sign that a business could possess a Moat.

   Free Cash Flow = Operating Cash Flow – Purchase of Property, Plant, and Equipment

3. **Is the Cash Dividends Paid to Free Cash Flow Ratio (CDP to FCF Ratio) below 1 throughout the years?**
   For dividend paying companies, the safest and most conservative source of dividends would be from a business's Free Cash Flow. Even though most dividend-investors would prefer to look at the Dividend Coverage Ratio, we feel that the CDP-to-FCF Ratio is a better gauge for a business's ability to continue paying dividends. The smaller the ratio, the more desirable it is in terms of safety of the dividends. A business that has a strong stream of cash flow in good as well as bad times can still afford to pay out dividends comfortably in times of economic distress. If the CDP-to-FCF ratio is low, even

if Free Cash Flow of the business falls in bad times, the company need not decrease the amount of dividends paid as the company can afford to pay out dividends from the cash it has accumulated in previous years and thus provide some form of cushion for its stock price as well. As Free Cash Flow increases throughout the years for a business with a durable competitive moat, the dividends that shareholders enjoy will move in tandem with Free Cash Flow growth. If you can find a fundamentally strong company with a good chance of having material increases in its Free Cash Flow in the future and that has a CDP to FCF Ratio that is low, chances are, the dividends you receive from the company will increase over time — that is the true magic of dividend paying companies.

CDP to FCF Ratio = Cash Dividends Paid / Free Cash Flow

Dividend Coverage Ratio = Dividends Per Share / Earnings Per Share

So, this is it. A 13-point checklist of various ratios and important figures that are gleaned from the three financial statements of a business that can provide a great picture of the overall profitability, financial stability and cash flow situation of the business. It will be rare to find a business that can fulfil all 13 points listed in the checklist so let the checklist be a guide for you. However, do not let it *dictate* your investment activities as you have to remember, The Story counts as well! We now move to Valuation — how to place a business value onto shares that can be radically different from its share price.

Important Questions to ponder about…

1. How do you think the income statement, balance sheet and cashflow statement are related?
2. What are some things which the financial statements will NOT tell you about the business?
3. Does it make sense to use the same metrics to compare businesses in different industries? Why or why not?

Appendix: Online Resources and Recommended Books

In the Introduction of our book, we mentioned how grateful we are to various professional investors and financial writers for penning down their precious thoughts and experiences on websites as well as book and other print-publications. We would now like to share them with you. Bear in mind that such lists can never be considered exhaustive and nothing would make us happier if you, the reader, can find precious resources to add to this list.

Good Online Resources

1. http://www.morningstar.com
2. http://www.investopedia.com
3. http://www.gurufocus.com
4. http://www.ycharts.com
5. http://buffettfaq.com
6. http://www.berkshirehathaway.com/letters/letters.html
7. http://www.wikinvest.com
8. http://www.fool.com
9. http://thefinance.sg

Recommended Books

1. *The Intelligent Investor* and *Security Analysis* by Benjamin Graham
2. *One Up on Wall Street* and *Beating the Street* by Peter Lynch
3. *Common Stocks and Uncommon Profits* and *Paths to Wealth through Common Stocks* by Phillip Fisher
4. *Five Rules for Successful Stock Investing* by Pat Dorsey
5. *The Neatest Little Guide to Stock Market Investing* by Jason Kelly
6. *Rule #1* by Phil Town

7. *The Financial Times Guide to Value Investing* by Glen Arnold
8. *Your Money and Your Brain* by Jason Zweig
9. *The Little Book of Behavioural Investing* and *Value Investing* by James Montier
10. *How to Read Financial Reports* by John Tracy

www.ingramcontent.com/pod-product-compliance
Lightning Source LLC
LaVergne TN
LVHW011812200926
848484LV00005B/1161